Richard Satterley
Carlton Design Consultants.
1975.

THE MANAGEMENT OF DESIGN SERVICES

THE MANAGEMENT OF DESIGN SERVICES

by J. NOEL WHITE

London
GEORGE ALLEN AND UNWIN LTD
RUSKIN HOUSE   MUSEUM STREET

Printed in Great Britain
in 11 point Times Roman type
by The Aldine Press, Letchworth

To Isa with love

Foreword
by the Earl of Drogheda, Chairman, *Financial Times*

The sound, but oversimplified, recipe for success in business is to have the right commodity available, at the right price, at the right time. To put into practice such a counsel of perfection requires a complex of skills, of which designing is one. The rightness of the product or service will depend on whether it successfully meets the common needs of a sufficient number of customers. Market research and sales experience, interpreted with a modicum of creative imagination, can provide the basis for product planning. But the realisation of the plan depends first and foremost on the effectiveness of the work of the design team. Responsibility for the effectiveness rests with managers who set the objectives, choose the designers, work out the instructions, assess the reliability of design solutions and commission the means of presenting the product to the customer. All these aspects are dealt with in this book.

Built into this chain of management decisions will be an effective system of control within which the designers will work to achieve an acceptable price. Making sure that the product reaches the market at the right time begins with the design process and continues through production and distribution.

The managing of design work in modern business has become a specialised skill which unfortunately is still not much considered in business schools, largely because so little published information has been collected and presented in a convenient form for the student of management.

The publication of this book, which brings together much of the experience of successful managers, previously available only in conference papers and magazine articles, removes that excuse. Its contents are relevant to a wide variety of managers in industry, commerce and public administration. The case studies which it records exemplify the principles of managing design work and will remain valid for many years. The author has had first-hand experience of design administration as Deputy Director of the Council of Industrial Design (now the Design Council); he organised with the *Financial Times* two National

Conferences on Design Management and as an editorial adviser to *Design* magazine was aware of most of the published work on the subject. I am confident that *The Management of Design Services* is a useful contribution to the study of this most important subject.

DROGHEDA

Acknowledgements

I owe so much to so many for the experience recorded in this book that it is difficult to do justice to them all, but first I must acknowledge my debt to my former colleagues at the Design Council, Sir Gordon Russell who was Director when I joined in 1954; Sir Paul Reilly, his successor; Mr Michael Tree who initiated this work with my publisher; Mr John Blake, now Head of Information and for many years Editor of *Design* magazine; and to his successor as Editor, Mr Corin Hughes Stanton.

I am also indebted to the Design Council and *Design* magazine for recording the wise words of those with whom I was associated in the organisation of conferences on design management when many of them were speakers: Professor Bruce Archer, Mr Alec Davis for the checklist on page 67 from the *Design* Supplement 'Print for Exporters', Professor Sir Misha Black, Mr Terence Conran, Sir Roger Falk, Mr R. D. Fairbairn, Mr Michael Farr, Dr D. Firth, Mr R. D. Ganderton of BEA, Mr Kenneth Grange, Mr Noel Jordan (including figures 16 and 17, and plate IV), Mr Leslie Julius, Sir William Mather, Sir Anthony Milward, Dr Alex Moulton, Sir Arthur Norman, Mr R. T. Reynolds (including the photographs on plate III), Mr John Sainsbury (including plate II) and Mr Norman Stevenson.

I gratefully acknowledge to the Production Engineering Research Association the extracts of texts and diagrams (figures 6 and 7) from the papers given to its conference 'Marketing Industrial Products' by Mr E. K. Ford, Mr P. J. Natsler, Mr G. H. Sugden, Mr R. A. Wenham and myself. For illustrations I must thank the Design Council (plates I and II), Mr F. H. K. Henrion (figures 13 and 14), Hille of London (figure 11), the former National Marketing Council (figures 1, 8, 9 and 10); and figures 2 and 3 are reproduced by permission of the Controller of Her Majesty's Stationery Office.

The book would never have reached completion without the encouragement of Mr Christopher Martin, and the help of Mrs E. Wessels who made the typescript from my tapes, Mrs E. W. Cheeseman who typed the index and Mr S. Garatti who relentlessly progressed the work.

Contents

Introduction

Up and coming managers are usually full of good ideas. It is a characteristic which marks them out for promotion. But a reputation for lively ideas must be matched by an ability to translate the idea into a successful reality. So often the 'ideas man' fails to become a 'results man' because he lacks the knowledge and skill to put his idea into a physical form which will make it effective in practice. We have all seen some ideas founder because the manner in which they are realised is muddled and inefficient. Not all ideas need a physical form, but very many do. A new pattern of work flow, for example, will involve a rearrangement of equipment and possibly the selection of suitable new office furniture; a proposal to improve a catering service may require a complete reorganisation of kitchen facilities and counter display as well as new literature and advertising to publicise it; a new technique for forming metal may suggest an extensive revision of a product range to make it more economical to produce and more attractive to the customer. In countless cases of this kind the linking activity which translates the acceptable idea into a marketable product or service is the process of designing. When a new idea is developed there inevitably comes a moment when the conception must be interpreted in terms of hardware, or print, or a series of objects in an appropriate environment. There is in fact a design problem which has to be managed.

In this sense designing is an activity which is organised by management in order to further the objectives of the enterprise. It is not so much a state of grace or a characteristic of respectability as a process whereby management gives visible form to ideas, so that the resultant meets a set of specific requirements. Frequently the manager does not realise that he is involved in the design process and so fails to enlist the appropriate skills at the right moments. In consequence he fails to obtain from the idea the optimum benefits. He may make do with unsuitable existing resources or consult several specialists without himself having the essential knowledge of design management needed to co-ordinate their separate recommendations, or without employing someone who has the synthesising skill which is required to organise the design activity.

When the manager accepts that designing is one aspect of problem solving, he will begin to develop his own ability to recognise the design aspects of any problem. In many concerns much effort is put into research and development without the basic realisation that as soon as research becomes development then designing begins and professional designers are required. If designers are only brought in at a later stage, their creative talents are necessarily circumscribed by the course of the earlier development. A company, for example, may become aware that its whole system of printed matter needs rationalisation and yet give instructions to printers without having the problem thoroughly appraised by a graphic designer. Substantial benefits in terms of variety reduction, simplification, clarity and impact can be lost through a failure to identify the design problem and deal with it professionally.

Putting a new business idea into practice is not so much a matter of adding together several new specialised skills; it is more often a task of integrating a number of individual solutions so that a more efficient system or assembly is created. This is a process of synthesis, not simple addition. It is much more exacting and satisfactory to achieve a neat and economical solution than to add together several unrelated solutions each made in watertight compartments.

When a young manager is promoted he is often chosen for his ability to manage change. Procedures have become cumbersome and out of date, new equipment is required and premises need reorganisation. He may succeed someone who has solved each problem as it came along, in isolation, so that eventually the procedures are an accumulation of unrelated links in the organisational chain. For example, manufacturing techniques have been allowed to remain labour intensive in a situation where the standard of skill is declining, recruitment is difficult and cost per man-hour high; or the product or service has not been adapted to the changing needs of the user and the presentation is ineffective in today's context of selling; or the paperwork has proliferated and needs rationalisation and co-ordination. In each of these problems is an area of design work to be identified and managed, such as the designing of new product ranges for new processes and materials, or the introduction of new ergonomic and convenience standards for the user, or the designing of new packaging and sales literature, or the devising of a new typographical system for all paperwork and print.

The lack of precise definitions is always a handicap to any discussion on design. I fancy the early architects had a similar problem until there was a general understanding of the difference between a builder and an architect. Today we are still a little confused about the difference between an engineer and a designer. The International Committee of Societies of Industrial Design in Stockholm in 1959 attempted to define the role of the industrial designer thus:

An industrial designer is one who is qualified by training, technical knowledge, experience and visual sensibility to determine the materials, construction, mechanism, shape, colour, surface finishes and decoration of objects which are reproduced in quantity by industrial processes. The industrial designer may at different times be concerned with all or only one of these aspects of an industrially produced object. The industrial designer may also be concerned with the problem of packaging, advertising, exhibiting and marketing when the resolution of such problems requires visual appreciation in addition to technical knowledge and experience. The designer of craft-based industries or trades where hand processes are used for production is deemed to be an industrial designer when the work produced to his drawings or models is of a commercial nature, is made in batches or otherwise in quantity and is not the personal work of the artist craftsman.

The pioneer of London's underground system had a neater definition of design as 'intelligence made visible' which is a conception worth dwelling upon when we are so often surrounded by inescapable evidence of a lack of intelligence made all too visible. Hepplewhite, reflecting on the same subject, observed that 'to unite elegance and utility and combine the useful with the agreeable has ever been considered a difficult but honourable task'. To Michelangelo design was simply the elimination of the superfluous. For our purpose perhaps the pedestrian Stockholm definition will serve as a point of departure.

The manager who can identify the area of design work and efficiently organise the professional resources to deal with it, is well placed to achieve a high degree of cost effectiveness for his organisation. If he can show that he is a 'synthesiser' rather than an 'accumulator' he is potentially one of those rare managers who can successfully put ideas into practice and exploit the benefits which flow from skilfully managing the design process. A manager with this synthetic approach to problem solving will become aware how much imaginative designing can con-

15

tribute to the main areas of his business, administration, production and marketing. In administration design skills can facilitate the organisation of information, its collection, its processing, its presentation and its retrieval; in production design skills create the precise form of the product so that it is economic to make and satisfactory to use; in marketing design skills are used to present and promote the product or service. The design process, therefore, applies to most activities, determining the physical form of both three- and two-dimensional objects; its successful management affects the performance of departments as diverse as the factory, the sales office and the accounts section.

When experienced designers describe their skill as problem solving, they reflect the essential nature of their training and practice which is directed towards analysis, synthesis, evaluation and presentation. To this process they bring a strong sense of direction towards turning an idea into a physical entity. They are concerned to convert requirements, usually commercial but sometimes social, into products or systems which satisfy those requirements. Hence the manager with new ideas needs to know the basic character of the design process, so that he can define requirements in such a way that maximum scope is given to designers who can then satisfy them in a form which gives optimum value to both the producer and the user.

This book is addressed to the manager who has some training or experience in management principles, but as yet has little practical knowledge of the function of the design process in business. It concerns the manager with his foot firmly on the promotion ladder, who knows the basic techniques of management and is concerned to manage change in a profitable manner. It explains the situations in design work where these techniques apply and where attitudes particular to design work should be adopted. It describes the preliminary stages of administrative organisation which precede the creative activity, and an effective pattern of management control to stimulate creative solutions and evaluate them. It deals specifically with the relationship between the professional manager and the professional (staff or consultant) designer so that it can be efficient and productive. The effective partnership of these two elements in industry, commerce and public administration, is a vital aspect of management, particularly in the current climate of change. In the following chapters the roles of the manager and the designer are defined so that satisfactory methods of working can be developed to

16

exploit the expertise of each, and minimise unproductive friction between two very different types of professional.

The subject is addressed to the manager and does not encourage him to become an amateur designer, but to define the design problem which has to be solved and choose wisely the design team to work out the solution. There are other works published for aspiring designers of which Dorothy Goslett's *The Professional Practice of Design* (Batsford, 1971) is perhaps the most practical. It is here assumed that designers know the task of their own trade and that the manager wishes to know how to select designers and deploy them in the most successful manner. In the clear understanding of the respective roles of manager and designer lies the key to this success. Inexperienced managers often confuse the statement of requirements in a design brief by injecting into it preconceived solutions which inhibit the design work. Even when the manager has trained himself to be strictly objective in setting out the problem he will find it difficult to assess the degree of innovation which is acceptable in the solution in terms of plant investment, technical training and market acceptance. To attempt to organise a product development programme or corporate identity programme without a general knowledge of the design process is one of the pitfalls which can threaten the career of the ambitious manager.

A lack of this knowledge can lead to one of two extreme attitudes. The first is the belief that designers work entirely by intuition and are inspired to find solutions through some unintelligible mystique. This fosters the assumption that the design process is only concerned with the superficial aspects of styling, and that for this very little basic information is needed since the designer's contribution is only required in the final stages of product development. The second belief is equally hazardous because it assumes that designers are second cousins to the Almighty, should never be confused by the facts and are best left alone to deal with all creative aspects of product development without the restraint of managerial control. Needless to say the optimum lies in neither extreme.

Like any other business activity the design process has to be integrated by management with many other aspects of the organisation, technical, financial and marketing, so that it makes the maximum contribution towards the objectives of the enterprise. One of the difficulties is that there is very little information on designing presented from the

17

point of view of a manager within a business organisation. What does exist is mostly scattered throughout periodicals and conference reports, the majority published over the years by the Design Council. Recently more attention has been given to the examination of design methods, but much of the published work concerns the professional design and research organiser rather than the manager. A wide variety of experience is, however, lodged with firms who have developed design work as an important aspect of profitability. Realising this, the Duke of Edinburgh instituted at the Royal Society of Arts, of which he is President, a series of Awards for Design Management which invites those who win them to share their experience publicly. I am therefore greatly indebted to British European Airways, to Sainsbury, to British Thornton and to Race Furniture, all of whom have received these Presidential Awards and to whom I am deeply grateful for the generous way in which they have supplied information on their methods of managing design for the case studies in this book.

In the small firm the young manager may find that there is either no experience of design management, or the centre of gravity for all design work lies with an enthusiastic director whose time will be strictly limited as far as educating junior colleagues is concerned. This book, therefore, describes the basic rudiments of managing the design activity so that the manager can comprehend the intentions of a design director and take effective action to realise design objectives. It should also help him to judge the stages when he must refer back to his director whom he may regard as the 'client' for the organisation's design work.

In the large firm the manager will be broadly aware of his organisation's design policy. He may have seen design directives concerning the presentation of products or services, print, publications or advertising; there may even be a design manual for the guidance of staff. The manager in these larger concerns will be helped to understand design policy and directives, and to interpret what action he should take himself. There are almost no training schemes for design managers as distinct from designers. When development programmes are initiated or entirely new procedures proposed, most managers are faced with design implications which they find difficult to evaluate. Even if they are shown the designer's brief, they are often unable to analyse it in such a way that they can assess how the proposals will affect in detail the working of their own departments. Senior managers will, however, expect constructive comments before the proposals are acted upon. Criticism after the new arrangements are operating is much less helpful, considerably less welcome and vastly more expensive to implement.

The cardinal difficulty is that most design proposals, by definition, are concerned with situations which do not yet fully exist. A new situation demands new designs with a view to improvement; they reflect the future as much as the past; they are coping with an element of uncertainty to which the designers apply their imagination and intuition in addition to their powers of rationalisation. The manager has to be able to evaluate the answers to these uncertainties and apply informed judgement as well as straight comparisons with the past. If, for example, a manager knows that a new system of office communication is designed to meet changed conditions, he must be prepared to accept design proposals which are substantially different from what he is used to. The changeover to a new system will not only require time and budgets and perhaps retraining, but careful persuasion will also be needed to sell the new designs to the staff.

Designers who do not cope with change will not be serving the manager well. So he will be anxious to choose designers who have imagination and creative ability to produce new ideas. He may find that such people are unlike his colleagues because they constantly question old assumptions and share the necessary degree of conviction concerning their solutions which enables them to bridge the credibility gap between present uncertainties and future success. The manager himself, therefore, needs some understanding and feeling for the creative process if he is to guide a design team to success. So it is helpful to know what characteristics to look for in productive designers and, having selected the appropriate talents, to manage the activity profitably rather than stultify it with administrative prejudices.

The design aspect of a manager's job can often be the most creative side of his work, bringing him into contact with creative minds and giving him a high degree of satisfaction in contributing to the progressive development of his organisation as it moves into the excitement and uncertainty of the future.

Chapter 1

Design as a Process in Business

Although every period is an age of transition the decade of the 1970s is proving to be a time of intense industrial reorganisation. Companies of differing experience and potential are being grouped together for production and marketing reasons. Consequently new forms of organisation are being established to rationalise investment and production and services, to create a more effective marketing strategy.

Throughout industry and commerce, methods of doing things which have gone unchallenged for generations are now being put under the microscope and subjected to the test of cost-effectiveness. As soon as management starts to initiate change, it has, whether it recognises it or not, a design problem on its hands. The design work through which some aspects of innovation are achieved is the outward and visible sign of the wind of change, and of the up-to-date thinking which is going on within an organisation.

In the days when designers were rare and neglected by all but the enlightened elite of industry, it was often said that a universal panacea for an ailing product range, a lame promotion and publicity programme or a confused corporate identity, was to engage the services of a trained designer. This remains an important initial step; but it is only the very beginning, because a management which is inexperienced in the managing of design services may not employ these services effectively. The first essential is to identify the design problems. Then there is the difficult and continuing task of managing the design process so that it effectively contributes to the profitability of the enterprise. Design work is ineffective when it is not aligned with company objectives or successfully integrated with the existing organisation. A company needs to know why it is employing designers, what it wants them to do and how their skills can be directed effectively.

One of the very salutary spin-offs from employing designers is that this experience forces management to think hard about the essentials of their business. Thinking hard is often an uncongenial activity even for management. It is more convenient just to be busy. Being busy gets you into less trouble than thinking hard; it can lull you into a feeling of job satisfaction, indeed into a feeling of job security. But, as Bismarck once acidly observed, 'any fool can be busy'. If you are busy there is no time left for thinking hard, you can daily withdraw exhausted to your domestic hearth with the mistaken conviction that business will be as usual tomorrow.

So involvement with designers and design activity can be a recognition not only that change is being coped with, but also that some fundamental thinking has taken place. The manager who has not seen a designer about for some time perhaps should be a little worried. Maybe he should look over his shoulder and discover what are the design policies of his competitors, or even more important what are the design success stories in parallel, rather than competing, industries. If you make office furniture, it would pay to keep a close eye on the design development of the communications industry and the change in the sociological attitudes of young women seeking clerical work. The future may lie not in desks and chairs, but in consoles and conveyor systems. The one certainty among all the uncertainties is that change, to a greater or lesser degree, must be faced, and that coping with change involves managing the design process. Consequently the wise firm has a continuing policy of innovation which relates to the use of new materials, the introduction of new processes and the changing requirements of present and future customers.

Innovation

Undue resistance to change is a dangerous attitude, as some illustrious firms which are no longer in business have found out too late. A planned programme of innovation, constantly reviewed, avoids the pitfall of stagnation and conditions the young manager to accept change as a matter of course. I remember discussing this point with a director of a leading management consultant firm; I was urging the need for all firms whether large or small to have a design policy. He thought for a moment, then said that all firms needed a policy for innovation; if they

21

had such a policy then they would inevitably find that they would be involved in design, because change eventually forces management to organise design work. This can be done in a professional or amateur fashion.

Change without carefully considered design work can frequently be a precious opportunity lost. Consequently a policy for innovation will have built into it an element of improvement of product or service which results in greater satisfaction for the user and higher profitability for the enterprise. The improvement will often be achieved by the skilful management of design services. To deny these design services to middle management, or to manage them inefficiently, is to forgo some of the benefits of change.

However it is not sufficient for management to approve in principle a policy of innovation. The key question is: how much? In the context of designing this is a very important assessment. Therefore an essential preliminary to a brief for design work is an indication of the degree of innovation which will be acceptable to the Board. This will be determined by the amount of investment which can be applied to new or modified plant and to retraining, by the forecast from market research concerning market acceptability; and finally, the point which is often ignored, by the ability of the sales force to sell the product or services. Regular visitors to the Design Centre will have observed that sometimes a lively small firm produces a bright design idea, but lacks the investment to manufacture sufficient quantity in order to make a profit or to promote the product energetically enough to ensure sufficient orders. After a discreet period a larger firm comes along exploiting the design idea in a modified form with adequate resources for production and promotion. Skilled design cannot bring home the bacon without skilled management, and the converse is often true, although ample resources can often compensate for lack of design skill, but at a lower rate of cost-effectiveness.

In a situation of change design work can be expected to contribute to higher benefits from existing resources (financial, plant, distribution, etc.), of greater operational efficiency in factory, office and transportation, of a more satisfactory working environment; to more effective promotion of the product or service to the customer, and to greater satisfaction of the customer's needs leading to higher profitability. Examples are given in the case studies in chapters 4 and 5, but here are some brief instances.

An improvement in the use of plant might be achieved in the manufacture of a mechanical pump if the design office were able to reduce the number of moving parts by 10 per cent. This might also lead to greater customer satisfaction because less maintenance would be required; which in turn might justify a 5 per cent increase in the selling price. The reduction of moving parts might also achieve a reduction in weight and volume which could lower the cost of distribution. Fewer parts also mean less storage of components and less documentation. Each saving may be small in itself, but in sum may make the difference between a competitive product and a loser. In another instance a designer might devise a new system of lighting for a factory which would improve the illumination of work areas and so increase accuracy and reduce fatigue, cutting down rejected work and raising output and pride in the job.

By designing a piece of furniture to pack flat in a carton there may be a marginal improvement in costs of production or assembly, but there may be a major saving in transport costs and in the storage space of the wholesaler and retailer. The carton itself may provide an opportunity for graphic design to publicise the product and tie in with advertising.

Design is fundamental and pervasive; it begins with the idea for a product to meet the market need, and it is concerned with production, distribution, promotion and after sales service. But it is only fully effective when it is skilfully managed so that the designers are designing *into* the product characteristics which rationalise production, enhance value, thus providing sales points, and designing *out* wastage in effort, materials and man hours.

Organisation

A report by the OECD following a survey of European design departments concluded that 'the designer's responsibility covers the whole process from the conception to the issue of the detailed drawings and specifications for production and its interest continues throughout the life of the product in service'. This confirms the often-repeated advice to management to bring in the design team at the beginning of a project and to give maximum scope to the development of the product in relation to the user. Designers are hardly ever product-complacent and almost always highly sensitive to human factors. Because designers are indefatigable students of how people use artifacts and how they react to

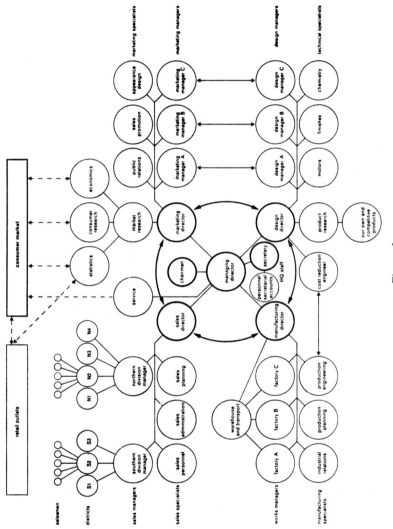

Figure 1

their environment, they should have a close relationship with the marketing director. As Sir Peter Tennant observed, 'marketing starts with the people and not with the product'. Firms which are heavily production-oriented often find it difficult to relate design work sufficiently to customers' satisfaction.

The National Marketing Council published a diagram (figure 1) which clearly shows the organisation of the design function in relation to marketing and manufacture. In this the design director's dialogue is primarily with marketing and manufacture, rather than with the sales director. This is a policy consideration of some importance. The first step towards using design services as one element in solving the problems of an enterprise, is for company policy to require that design work directly contributes to marketing.

As the manager looks at the usual pyramidal chart of his organisation he sees a simple triangle with the managing director at the apex. Below, the position is not simple. The departments fan out, subdivide and inter-relate in some profusion.

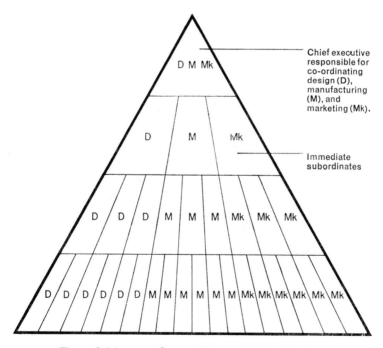

Figure 2 Diagram of a possible organisation structure

The impression it gives appeals to those at the top of the pyramid; it looks tidy and impressive. For those in the second quarter of the pyramid the picture is distorted because the sectors in the chart are of different sizes and the progression of their work moves on different timescales as a PERT chart will show. It may, therefore, be helpful if for the purposes of design management the chart is drawn not as a pyramid but as an interrelation of quadrangles whose sides taper at different degrees. For a given project this gives a better idea of the inter-relationship of the main departments at any given time in the development of a project. It shows the stable triangle imposed at the top which is concerned with policy and strategy; below, in this case, are the three principal divisions of activity as set out in the Board of Trade Export Handbook No. 3. Below the policy triangle the design activity is initially large but, as it reaches its objectives, the management of the manufacturing activity overtakes it, and that in turn is superseded by the marketing activity. Eventually the particular product range which has been designed will pass maturity and begin to wane and marketing will press for a new design programme. Consequently the relationship of the activities will change again. In real life the situation is even more dynamic because departments are undertaking more than one project at a time, so that the manager is concerned not only with keeping the activities within a project in phase, but also with maintaining a balanced relationship between projects in order to spread the load adequately.

Companies have great difficulty in charting the relationship between departments in a manner which reflects the real life situation. Most charts illustrate wishful thinking and symmetrical geometry rather than what really happens. The symmetry of some charts may in fact hinder a fruitful relationship between different departments. If the manager suspects that this is happening it is better to abandon the neat drawings than to hamstring progress. However, a chart is useful for defining relationships and making them apparent to those who have to make them work, even if it has to be oversimplified for that purpose. Such charts are not capable of much precision and when they become too elaborate they stray too far from actuality to be helpful. Many charts show parity of salary levels rather than equivalents in actual responsibility and activity.

The manager may have the initial task of persuading at least one member of the Board that this should be a declared aspect of company

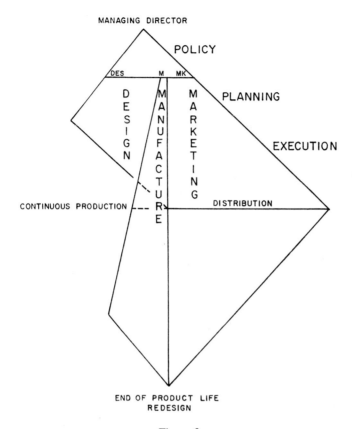

Figure 3

policy. To do this it may be necessary to cite examples where design work has contributed notably to success (see chapter 5). When the Board has accepted the policy there is a real challenge to the manager to justify the decision by the successful organisation of design work in his own firm. He is then faced with the task of stating clearly the problem, identifying the contribution of design work and programming the activity.

Much valuable work has been done by Professor J. Christopher Jones at Manchester University and by Professor L. Bruce Archer at the Royal College of Art, London, to demonstrate that a large area of design work is capable of systematic organisation. The traditional idea that intuition is the main ingredient in the design recipe is no longer

27

attractive. So much information is now needed to define the problem, the choice of the optimum materials and processes is so wide and the market so complex, that a systematic approach to designing is essential. It remains true, however, that a crucial stage of the design process is creative. At that point a designer's intuition, which must be highly developed, is vital. It can be argued that any problem in which all the aspects can be strictly quantified, is really a calculation and not a design problem. One of the most difficult tasks for the manager is to identify the stages to which precise data can be applied, and the stage of uncertainty where a creative leap has to be taken.

All systematic approaches to design work follow the now classic sequence of

(*a*) statement of requirements,
(*b*) collection of information,
(*c*) analysis and synthesis into a new solution,
(*d*) selection and evaluation,
(*e*) communication.

A trained manager will not be daunted by (*a*) the statement of requirements, nor (*b*) the collection of relevant information, nor yet by (*e*) the communication of the solution for the executive action. But the creative stage of (*c*) analysis and synthesis will usually present him with an unfamiliar and vital problem. The core of the whole activity is the synthesis of the requirements with the means available, to obtain an optimum solution. All stages must be conditioned by this essential concern.

Statement of Requirements

The statement of requirements has the dual function of initiating the design activity and monitoring it in the later stages. The manager treats the statement as an essential tool and devotes meticulous care to its preparation and acceptance by senior management. He cannot expect that an immaculate and inviolate document will result, but he can impress on all concerned that once the statement is agreed, deviation from it will cost money. His own starting-point will be a statement of 'product *policy*' by top management; this will circumscribe the design brief and the 'product *programme*' which will be undertaken by managers. All design work subsequently done will be within the framework of this statement, the approval of which is a clear-cut boardroom responsibility. To embark on full-scale design work without it is to risk the failure of conforming with company objectives.

The first task of this stage is to establish with the marketing director what market need the new product or service is intended to meet. Market research is a valuable indication of the immediate past, but some imaginative and informed future forecasting is needed if the new product is to have the maximum effective life in the market. The trend of sales graphs and relevant sociological statistics concerning distribution of population and income and buying habits can help to project the future. The market need can be examined in terms of pure function (how something should work) and of human factors such as ergonomics and appearance, but at this stage it is not yet necessary to examine in depth. The marketing men will, however, make some appraisal of what degree of innovation is likely to be accepted by the market. Leonardo da Vinci's notebook is full of brilliant ideas for which the market was not then ripe.

Thus the need may be for a new bicycle which any member of the family may use by instant adaptation, mother or daughter, father or son, which is capable of carrying shopping parcels stably fore and aft, and which can itself be put into the boot of a car so that it is available away from home. It was such a need that Dr Alex Moulton was aiming to meet when he designed the Moulton Stowaway bicycle. From this statement of requirements stemmed many technical problems such as a new physical structure for the frame, the development of a tyre suitable for the small wheel and appropriate systems of suspension, braking and gear changing. All the technical development served the statement of requirements which was the starting-point. Techniques are only valuable when they meet specific needs. The production engineer who is casting about for an excuse to use a new technique may be invaluable, but the manager will keep a watchful eye on him to ensure that it serves an identifiable need.

Collection of Information

Having arrived at a statement of requirements which is acceptable to the Board and falls within its policy for product development, it is worth

29

reviewing afresh, with the designers, the products on the market which already make some attempt to meet the requirements. There may be some useful lessons to be learnt which were not so apparent before the statement of requirements had been undertaken. If this examination does not change the situation, then a programme of data collection can be organised.

At this point the manager will become sensitive to the expenditure of one of the most valuable commodities, *time*. So he will need to have a crude idea of total span of design, production and initial distribution. Within this broad assessment of time, which will inevitably be subject to modification as more precise information becomes available, he can set a limit to the period of data collection. This is vital because collecting data can go on indefinitely; it is an unexacting accumulative business, its by-ways are endless and sheer bulk is often mistaken for the yardstick of success. It is, moreover, a comfortable buffer from the uncomfortable and exacting activity of analysis and subsequent synthesis. It is, therefore, a difficult managerial task to confine data collection to the relevant, and limit the time. Experienced judgement is really the only guide. To make the period too long is to waste money and risk being overtaken by competitors. To make the period too short is to risk omitting some information essential to the long-term success of the product. The process of collection, therefore, has to be reviewed constantly and it would be wise to set the target date at the minimum, but to keep a flexible attitude towards extending the period. Perhaps the most important aspect is to maintain a sense of urgency.

In these two preliminary activities of (*a*) stating requirements and (*b*) information gathering, the manager is the central figure. In a well-ordered house access to library services and market research reports will already be routine, not requiring organising *ab initio* for each project. Managerial judgement is, however, needed to set the boundaries for desk and field research. Professor Bruce Archer has set down a cost for this effort at between 5 and 10 per cent of the total project. Certainly management needs to worry if, in conventional situations, the cost is substantially above this. Judgement is also needed to make clear to the design team the area of facts on the one hand, and the area of assumptions on the other on which the definition of the design problem is based. Subsequent analysis may show that a few of the facts were irrelevant, although not false and that some of the assumptions were false although not irrelevant. Such an outcome need not disturb management unduly. But if the facts are false and the assumptions irrelevant then there is more cause for concern.

These two preliminary stages (*a*) and (*b*) are mainly the concern of policy makers and managers who form the administrative core of the enterprise. Their intention is to set the stage adequately for an intensive creative activity by highly trained professionals whose efforts should not be complicated by deep involvement in the administrative preparations. Consultation will, of course, be needed and a simple expedient is to have a small policy group or central planning unit of top management to initiate these preliminary stages and provide the focus of consultation with senior colleagues, until the definitions are precise (which should be a short process) and the sources of information identified (which may take longer). When both are complete the emphasis of the project begins to change from administration at the end of stage (*b*) to creativity as the task of analysis begins at stage (*c*). In preparation for this, the policy group needs to hand over to designers, production engineers and marketing men who will form the design team responsible for the next two stages (*c*) and (*d*) of synthesis and the selection of the optimum solution. The policy group in a modified form will come into action again at the stage of evaluation (figure 4).

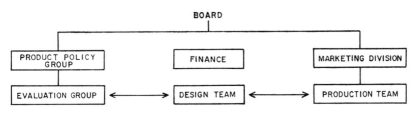

Figure 4 Organisation of Design Work

Analysis and Synthesis

Although the techniques of analysis are carried out by the design team, the manager must familiarise himself with the charts and check lists which are created as the main problem is divided into sub-problems and the relationship between them established. The manager's own time chart will reflect the sequence in which the sub-problems are tackled, so that he will be able to discover when a particular sub-problem is holding up the whole project. His own contribution will be to keep the activity goal-oriented and ensure that when the network of the sub-problems changes, his own timetable is adjusted. An excellent example of a comprehensive check list is given in Professor Bruce Archer's 'Systematic Methods for Designers' published by *Design* magazine.

At this stage it is important for the manager to understand the design process in order to be able to stimulate and encourage it without inhibiting it by too much administrative constraint. The controlling factor is that the activity is now synthetic, ranging over the field of requirements, surveying all the relevant data put forward, assessing the capability of the production techniques available and the characteristics of the available materials, some of which may be new both to the designers and the production engineers, and always relating them finally to the satisfaction of the user.

The manager's role is to ensure that all these balls are kept in the air without trying to juggle with them himself, encouraging the creative new solution, but always satisfying himself that any potential solution spans the range of requirements, not least the financial budget. His inevitable temptation is to introduce preconceived notions into the mix, thus reducing the chances of real innovation which can result in market leadership. Admittedly there is very little known about creative ability, but one of its characteristics is the ability to associate things which have not previously been associated (see page 111). Consequently designing which is confined to reshuffling existing solutions is unlikely to result in any major advance. Some managers are prone to reject unusual solutions without sufficient objective examination, which is, at the least, discouraging to a design team, particularly if the solution in fact conforms closely to the statement of requirements. The manager may, perhaps, be implying that the solution is too novel for acceptance by the market at present without massive promotion which cannot be afforded; this is a valid argument. Salesmen, however, are apt to be double-faced about innovation. Their customers are always glibly asking them for something new and the salesmen feed this back to management as a firm requirement, but when faced with a product which is unfamiliar and unlike any competitor's product, they tend to become highly conservative, protesting that it will not sell. Introduction of new lines to salesmen should therefore be carefully planned as an operation in order to explain how the new design characteristics can be used as sales points (see chapter 2).

Thus the role of the manager at this stage changes subtly from the organisation man towards that of the impresario dealing with creative talent (figure 5). His eye is fixed on the objectives and his encouragement is goal-directed, but he recognises the delicate nature of designing and avoids creating stagnation by over-managing. In fostering the optimum conditions he is often obliged to restrain his senior colleagues from interfering too much, but as promising lines of thought develop he is quick to stimulate the interest of the production people and then the marketing department. One of his constant preoccupations is to heighten the awareness and powers of observation of staff designers, encouraging them to widen their experience through contact with new exhibitions of both science and art, with books and magazines and with stimulating minds at conferences and seminars. Dullness in the design department may be criticism of management.

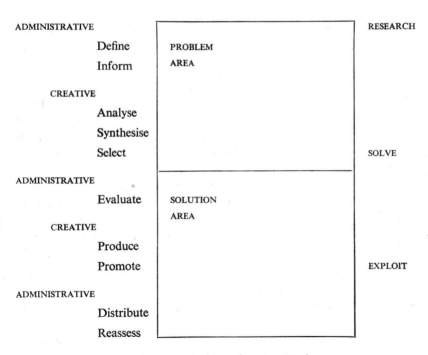

Figure 5 Analysis of Design Work

The easiest way for the manager to integrate himself into this stage is to adopt the role of scorer, charting the development of design ideas as formally as possible, checking their advantages against the list of requirements and making sure that the trend is always towards synthesis. If after several weeks the ideas are still generalised and wide-ranging, rather then becoming more precise and narrowing towards the objectives, then it is time to intervene, tactfully but firmly. Usually there is no absolute solution which must be pursued regardless of time and expense. Most requirements are capable of being met by several differing solutions. The aim of the synthetic stage is, therefore, to arrive at one or two strong runners which are worth examining in depth. The designers, of course, may find an answer which they are convinced is the optimum. It may then be necessary to move smartly into stage (d) of selection and evaluation. If you are lucky the designers' hunch will be proved right; if not the process has to be recycled back to stage (c). This flexibility is essential if the design team is not to become stale; and it is worth remembering that none of the stages need to be regarded as watertight compartments.

When performing this role of the impresario, the manager may find it an advantage that he is not a professional designer. He will be respected and relied upon for his expertise in organisation, but he will not be regarded as a competitor in the creative process. A few distinguished designers do assume the managerial role but they sometimes attract the assumption that they are designers manqué and at the same time lack the professional administrative skills. Consequently they are weak on both legs. Successful design managers do, however, arrive from both disciplines.

In most cases the manager's function will be to reinforce the systematic approach and the methodology without squeezing out the contribution of inspired intuition. He will find the works of Professor Bruce Archer and Professor Christopher Jones particularly helpful in developing these systematic techniques which he can apply if his design team is not familiar with them. But the methods without the creative talent are not sufficient, and they do not of themselves turn a manager into a designer. In a small enterprise the manager may have to contribute much of the systematic approach; in a large concern he will become the co-ordinator of such systems, an example of which is given in figure 7.

34

Selection and Evaluation

Let us presume that several solutions which seem feasible have emerged. It will then be necessary to establish which is the optimum by a process of evaluation. The manager can give a rating to the various aspects in the statement of requirements. In an appliance the ability to carry out work efficiently, reliability, and ease of operation and assembly may be the important factors in that order. In a range of domestic light fittings function and appearance are both of great importance, appearance often taking precedence in the user's mind. The working out of a system of rating some of the aspects can be quantified like economics and time factors; others are subjective such as appearance, although none the less real and important. A useful way of tackling this is to adopt the classics masters' methods of marking essays, e.g. Alpha plus $(\alpha+)$, Alpha (α), Alpha minus $(\alpha-)$, Beta plus $(\beta+)$, Beta (β), Beta minus $(\beta-)$ and Gamma plus $(\gamma+)$, Gamma (γ) and Gamma minus $(\gamma-)$. In this way Beta can be taken as the standard of the existing product against which the new design is being compared. The graduation of nine steps is usually sufficient at this stage.

At this time the design team organises preliminary drawings including perspectives for discussion and then models which can be subjected to basic tests of performance, reliability and convenience, and can be analysed in detail by production. The project now reverts again to its administrative character with the manager firmly controlling the activity. It is now necessary to report progress to the wider interests of finance and marketing represented in the policy group, for whom the design team must prepare, in addition to measured drawings, sketches and working models which can be understood by the non-engineers. Otherwise discussion may be frustrated, if not acrimonious, losing much time and goodwill. The design team leader must be able to explain the various solutions, describing their merits and snags if any. A designer's ability to sketch quickly and clearly emphasising essential characteristics is a great advantage. If this skill is not available the camera can be used in advance of a meeting to highlight some of the characteristics of the model more realistically than even a model itself can show to a group of people, particularly to set it into its context or environment as might be the case with a room heater.

With the policy group's consent, the responsibility now passes to the

35

evaluation group and the task of the manager is to acquaint the members with the essentials of each solution before detailed discussion takes place with the design team. This allows useful consultation outside the group. The evaluation group will meet several times, calling for appropriate test information and possibly test marketing reports. It narrows the alternatives down to one or two possible solutions and may recycle them back to stage (c) for further consideration. Members of the group will find check lists useful in order to make valid comparisons and fairly elaborate costings and production studies may be required before a final recommendation can be made to the Board asking it to back the most favoured solution.

Throughout this stage presentation of information is vitally important, The manager makes sure that the optimum solution is not rejected because it has been inadequately explained and comprehended. Such an outcome is a great waste of expenditure and often undermines the morale of the design team. One of the safeguards against this is to make sure from the start that sufficient budgets are available for the actual designing. Often budgets are constructed on the basis of the physical production and distribution of the product. The costs of researching and designing have to be scrounged from the advertising or consultancy budgets. The scope of the design work is then restricted and the presentation of results in particular is inadequate.

Another failing is that insufficient care is given to the preparation of vital information for the evaluation group. The facts are often not correctly marshalled and statistics not clear. This is a fault of design management and deserves study in order to get the best results out of design work. Some consultant designers are most professional in their presentations because they realise the risk of failure at this stage. In order to support thorough presentation, there must be the right equipment such as projectors (slide, epidiascope, overhead), boards, chalks, display paper, felt pencils, lighting, etc. An inefficient presentation can be a disaster which dissipates confidence in design work. On the other hand there is also a danger if a session turns out to be all presentation and no content.

Evaluation can become a dogfight if not skilfully stage-managed. All interested parties converge on the suggested solution and unless care is taken the situation can become a destructive skirmish. The manager's concern will be to keep it constructive and make his own contribution objective. The marketing side will become actively involved, and the salesmen apprehensive. The production engineers will concentrate on the snags which have to be ironed out and may be worried by the degree of retooling required and the consequent delay. A hint of delay will further disconcert the marketing men. Accountants will resent the outlay and the risk. So it needs an iron managerial nerve to steer the project through these troubled waters towards a positive development.

The manager furthermore will have to be careful to protect the design team from an overdose of random criticism, while avoiding the impression that the designers are being excluded from essential discussion. The manager's personal ability to manage people as well as information is severely taxed at this stage. His ability to remain the wise guide, philosopher and friend to all can well safeguard the investment in effort. But he must be prepared when his objective judgement dictates to recommend to the policy group a recycling back to stage (c), if the evaluation points to fundamental weaknesses in the solution. He then has the difficult job of putting it across to the design team without losing their enthusiasm for a fresh start. He will find this easier if he has from the first discouraged an attitude of 'absolutism' to which some designers are addicted.

The vulnerability of the project during evaluation is one reason why administrative responsibility at this stage reverts to the policy group. The process of evaluation may throw up some critical decisions concerning pros and cons which seem equally balanced. In such a situation the lack of clear-cut advantages will raise doubts about the viability of the solution. The policy group may not be unanimous and the matter may have to be referred to the Board. The wary design manager will have foreseen this possibility and will already have kept the most appropriate Board member in touch with the main developments of the project so that he is quickly able to understand the background to the problem and assess the significance of the arguments for or against. With the particular assistance of a Board member who sees the issue partly from the inside, the Board will find it easier to discuss the issues among themselves and maybe take a justifiable risk in backing a degree of innovation which some of the evaluation group find disconcerting.

A Board which has a longstanding design policy and has given senior management a clear responsibility for the exploitation of creative design work, will probably have already agreed that one Board member with a particular aptitude for design shall be the spokesman for design matters. The term 'design director' is becoming quite frequent, not only in engineering firms but also in companies producing consumer goods. In a firm which has not yet reached this stage, some pressure from the managers can engender a rudimentary equivalent. The design manager may find it convenient to feed design matters tactfully into one of the directors and create a special relationship, making sure not to upset the hierarchy. Those directors who are in favour of backing change are usually not difficult to identify.

Difficulties inevitably induce delays, and if the manager is not energetic, the project is likely to become bogged down. Precious weeks can be lost and if the ultimate decision is that the solution is unsound and the problem must be recycled, then the delay could be serious. The moment of maturity is not very long. In fast-moving markets it can be embarrassingly short. So the manager must have his timetable under frequent review and he may find that he alone will have to force the pace, because his colleagues are so engrossed in the detail of their own problems. He will constantly be drawing attention to the time factor as the evaluation studies pile up one upon another. Like data collection, evaluation is never quite complete, so the manager, ever watchful on the bridge, will have to gauge the moment when the ladder must be pulled up and he must summarise the situation for the Board.

There are those who can remember when the art of the précis was taught in schools. At the time it seemed boring and even destructive when elegant passages of prose were put on the chopping-block. But the ability to put a problem in a nutshell is a cardinal virtue in a design manager, and the tedium of learning the art is amply compensated by the mental discipline which it fosters and the recognition it receives from the decision makers on the Board. Designers in general tend not to be highly articulate. Their talents are deployed in other directions. Nor are they assiduous in keeping records. Their thoughts are bent upon the future rather than the immediate past. So they are not always good at recapitulating and thus avoiding those wide-ranging discussions with higher authority concerning what they have done, and therefore need not do again, and what they have not done and therefore may well do now in order to reach their solution. The manager, on the other hand, must be skilled in this sort of verbal synthesis. His methodical approach

Chart of Responsibilities

Board	Define I (*a*) Problem (*b*) resources and budgets
Policy Group	Inform II (*a*) State facts and Assumptions (*b*) collect data (*c*) indicate boundaries
Design Team	Analyse III (*a*) Relate definitions to characteristics (*b*) decide direction of inquiry (*c*) define crucial difficulties (*d*) divide into sub-problems
	Synthesise IV (*a*) Concentrate on creativity (*b*) solve (*c*) recycle
	Select Solution V (*a*) Search for optimum relationship of product cost to value (*b*) establish feasibility (*c*) confer with Production (*d*) prepare sketches and models
Evaluation Group	Evaluate VI (*a*) Apply scale of merit (*b*) test against brief (*c*) check cost and production ability (*d*) test market
	Communicate VII (*a*) Inform departments of solution (*b*) receive comment and assess (*c*) seek Board approval (*d*) order final drawings
Production Team	Produce VIII (*a*) Evolve Product and Tooling programme (*b*) pass back production models to Evaluation Group
Marketing Division	Promote IX (*a*) Prepare Marketing Plan, packaging, presentation, advertising, point of sales aid, publicity
	Distribute X (*a*) Instruct sales force
	Reassess XI (*a*) Examine feedback (*b*) recycle for modification

to the whole business will ensure that he can summarise the state of the game whenever the managing director chooses to drop his hat.

Let us, however, assume that all goes well. The reports from the marketing men are encouraging, the finance department can find no serious error in the costings, the production engineers have ingeniously overcome the major snags and the designers have not had second thoughts in favour of a much more advanced brainchild. Consequently the evaluation group is satisfied and the product programme goes forward to the Board for approval and gets it with a solemn warning about cost inflation. The design manager heaves a sigh of relief. He has negotiated the first administrative stage of setting up the project, he has acted as midwife to the hazardous creative process and he has raised the baby through the stresses and strains of evaluation. The solution has now to be communicated to all concerned, the product made and the path to the customer prepared. He is more than half-way home in effort but somewhat less perhaps on the time chart.

Communication

Before communicating the solution to all concerned, it is wise to take stock of all aspects of the project in order to make sure that no part of the programme is out of line. The evaluation group will have gone over most of the ground, but their conclusions may have altered some details. It is most likely that under pressure from finance, the production engineers have achieved some cost reduction by value analysis; the design team on the other hand may have made consequent changes on the basis of cost-effectiveness, improving the product with only a partial reduction in cost of manufacture. The improvement may, however, have beneficial effects outside the production line as Sir William Mather has emphasised, such as less parts to store, re-order and replace; less administration in their collection and assembly; a shorter parts list, less variety in outside purchases, less inspection time, less book work. All these subtractions and additions have to be analysed and the budgets adjusted up and down accordingly, before a clear statement of the resources required can be circulated.

It is always difficult to cost and quote for a product which is still only at the design stage. Dr Alex Moulton recommends a method of setting weight targets for the groups and the whole, keeping running checks all the time. He makes a diagram of the colour-coded and tabulated whole, and then the budgeted and calculated weights are inserted, in the knowledge that certain types of mechanisms and constructions should have certain broad costs per pound according to their com-

40

plexity. Then the estimate of cost can be made. This method can work well for engineering products.

Having reconciled the costs (figure 6), a similar check can be made on the time-table, charting the completion of the various tasks in relation to the overall production plan. The final stages will be co-ordinated within the marketing division who will have requirements for packaging, handbooks and print of all kinds which cannot be specified until the design solution is reasonably advanced. These should be envisaged when the evaluation is finalised, although much of the design work for them will go ahead during the manufacture of the product. Even so print requirements should be included in the information circulated to the departments concerned. When all the checks have been reconciled, the complete information can be processed. The design decisions will usually be communicated in the form of drawings which will be worked into their final form by the design team in close collaboration with pro- duction engineers. Associated with these will be complete schedules covering parts, costs, etc. This is routine work for which the manager relies on the appropriate department to compile quickly and accurately.

Communicating the plans for a new product is more than just circu- lating drawings, models and schedules to all concerned. There is the managerial task of creating enthusiasm for the new product or service, explaining the objectives which it will fulfil and its merits compared with the old range and competitors' models. The support of the sales force is critical and a special presentation for them with senior manage- ment present is usually worthwhile at the communication stage because it can raise the temperature at the right moment. Salesmen who under- stand why a product is designed as it is, have a much better chance of selling it convincingly, and no salesman likes to be the last to hear all about it. Sources for enthusiasm are always valuable to salesmen and the design process can provide useful ammunition for the sales drive. A product may do less well because a thorough explanation of its design characteristics has not been given to those who have to sell it.

Consistent with industrial security, the communications network should be wide rather than narrow, and at the right moment a digest from the house magazine can lift morale. In most firms there are many sections which find difficulty in identifying themselves with the main effort of the organisation. The designing and launching of a new product range is an opportunity to identify all departments with the firm's

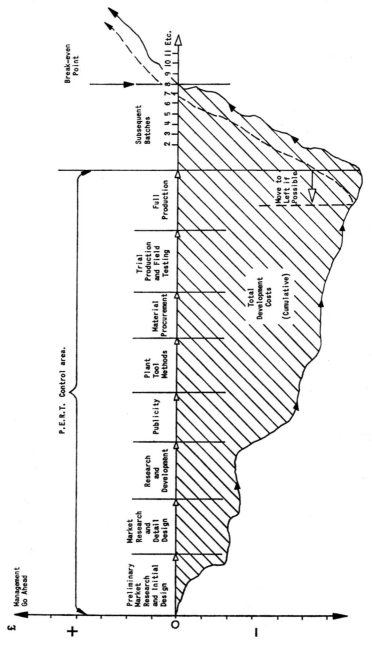

Figure 6

progress. Staff parties are often attended in greater strength by the departments who are remote from company objectives. This is probably because they feel isolated and want to identify more closely with the main stream of the firm's activities. Design work is essentially creative and innovatory and its output can be used to involve all personnel in the more exciting aspects of the enterprise. It is often necessary for the manager to seek an occasion to point out to routine sections their contribution to the effort and emphasise that their part is appreciated by management. The firm that achieves a design consciousness throughout its personnel is usually a lively, interesting, well-managed organisation.

Production

In theory the main task of designing is complete when the solution has been finalised for production, but it is rare for a design solution to require no modification at all during the process of manufacture. Most of the bugs will have been eliminated from the design during the stages of synthesis and evaluation when prototypes and models have been developed, but some allowance must be made for minor changes during preliminary production. When a change is necessary it is most important that the production team, now in charge of the project, should not improvise, but should consult with the design team. All modifications, however small, have a habit of affecting other aspects of the product, its print or its packaging. While a modification may solve the immediate problem, it equally may impair perhaps the performance, the appearance or access for maintenance. Consequently any proposal to modify should be reported to the design manager who would have to use his judgement whether the result should be submitted to the evaluation group. Normally this will not be necessary unless the alteration changes some design characteristics of the product. In every case it makes for good relations between the design team and the production team if modifications are treated as a joint responsibility. There is a great temptation for the production team to go it alone at this stage, but this may not produce the best results, nor a happy ship, and the manager will emphasise the joint nature of the responsibility from the start.

During production there is a tendency for matters to be left entirely to the production team and for the lines of communication to dry up. This is undesirable because there is work going on in parallel by other

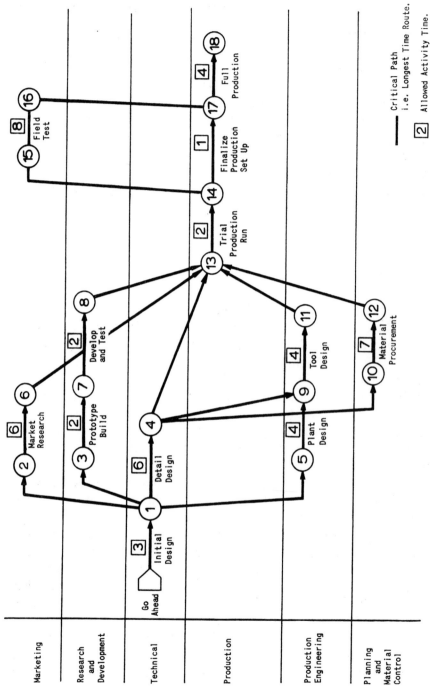

Marketing

Research and Development

Technical

Production

Production Engineering

Planning and Material Control

Go Ahead — ③ — Initial Design — ①

Detail Design ⑥

Market Research ⑥

Prototype Build ②

Develop and Test ②

Plant Design ④

Tool Design ④

Material Procurement ⑦

Field Test ⑧

Trial Production Run ②

Finalize Production Set Up ①

Full Production ④

—— Critical Path i.e. Longest Time Route.

② Allowed Activity Time.

Figure 7

departments to support the design and manufacture. So the policy group needs to meet occasionally to make sure that there is full co-ordination between marketing production and finance. In normal circumstances their meetings will be spaced out so that they will become target dates for the reporting of substantial progress. Day to day co-ordination and monitoring is the manager's job; too frequent intervention of the senior management can be counter-productive, and smacks too much of the bosses breathing down the necks of the chaps doing the work. Committees are no substitute for clear definitions of responsibilities and efficient communication. A prime objective is to minimise the period of manufacture in order to achieve prompt deliveries.

The policy group, acting as the central planning unit, will review anticipated dates of delivery, quantities and reorder levels, schedules for bought-in parts and by means of data processing keep production in step. Nowadays many design solutions are so complex and market requirements so diverse that production is controlled by scientific techniques involving computers. The company may also have a policy of sub-contracting for parts because this is cheaper, thus complicating the co-ordination and control. Production management is a study on its own, subsequent and complementary but apart from design management.

As soon as the first pre-production batch is available, tests can be carried out. When the first results come in, one concern of the design manager is to distinguish as soon as possible between comments due to design and those due to quality control. For example, a handle coming loose on a heavy saucepan after sustained use may be due to faulty design of the junction between handle and pan. On the other hand it may be that a non-corrosive screw was specified by the designers, but an ordinary screw used in production due to lack of quality control. The defect becomes apparent only after sustained use. In complicated structures the distinction between quality control and design can be significant.

The most effective method of expressing the time factor and controlling the programme is to use the critical path planning technique (figure 7). It indicates immediately when critical dates are overridden so that failures can be promptly tackled. But the method is only satisfactory if the manager keeps it up to date.

Promotion and Distribution

The interest of the marketing men is sustained throughout the process of design and manufacture, because they inherit the product. In planning distribution and promotion they become actively concerned. They will already have argued for certain design characteristics which make distribution, selling and servicing more effective. Now it is for them to organise the chain of distribution and equip the sales force with ancillary aids of packaging, print and advertising. We are concerned here with the design aspects of these requirements rather than general administration. Manufacturers of some products such as food and cosmetics are meticulous in their attention to packaging and advertising; other industries are only beginning to discover how great a part these can play in the success of their business.

Packaging is now a science in itself and the manager needs to know which of the many new developments can solve his problems. But the first essential is to know exactly how the product will be transported, stored and presented for sale and ultimate use. As systems of distribution and storage become more sophisticated, so the requirements for packaging become stricter. These affect dimensions, weight, climatic protection, security and the display of information. Consequently the manager will in a modified form apply to the packaging the stages of design activity which have already been applied to the product, e.g. statement of requirements, collection of information, analysis, synthesis, evaluation and communication. Not only is effective packaging itself a significant part of the investment, failure to package effectively can undermine the effort put into design and production. Packaging can not only ensure safe and prompt delivery in mint condition, but at all stages promote the firm and the product energetically. The realisation of these requirements economically is a considerable challenge to the manager.

Having defined the problem and collected the relevant data the task can then be turned over to the designer. In large firms there may be sufficient variety of products coming forward to justify a fully fledged packaging section in the design department. In that case the work will neatly fall within the control of the organisation, and the drill already described will apply in outline. Often, however, packaging skills will be commissioned from outside in order to reduce overheads and to ensure up-to-date knowledge is available. There are three main ways of doing this; to commission a consultant packaging designer; to allocate the work to an advertising agent with a packaging design service or to deal with a commercial packaging producer. It is the manager's job to find out which suits his own firm's situation best (see chapter 2).

Commissioning a consultant packaging designer can be the most direct and effective method provided you find a really talented designer and exercise methodical control of cost and time. The Design Council has a well-tried designer selection service which helps the manager to find the most appropriate designer. Using your own design consultant has the advantage of having an expert who has ranged across a wide field of packaging problems, and who from the professional standpoint is dedicated to solving your particular problem in the optimum manner from your point of view, and with the greatest originality acceptable to you. Working with consultants requires some managerial skill and a realisation that both parties are investing in each other. Thus results usually improve with time up to the point where either side becomes stale. The problems of dealing with consultant designers are discussed in chapter 3.

Most firms will already have a close relationship with an advertising agent, many of whom are large enough to support a comprehensive packaging department. The manager will go into this thoroughly in order to satisfy himself that adequate resources are available and that there is sufficient design talent to ensure an original solution which exactly meets his requirements. A stock answer may not give him maximum effectiveness. If the advertising agent has himself to go out to the design consultant, the manager will consider whether he would do better to do that himself. On the other hand there can be great merit in having the closest co-ordination between packaging and advertising, so that each exploits the impact of the other and relates to the other forms of print. A skilfully drawn contract with the advertising agent covering all these aspects can make a tidy co-ordinated service for the manager and keep costs under easy control. He will, however, make sure that he is getting the quality of design work which he is expecting.

If the manager decides to go direct to the packaging producer, he must be sure that he knows exactly what he wants, and that he can recognise it when he sees it. If so he can deal with several packaging producers on the basis of his own statement of requirements and then choose the contract which is most attractive from all aspects, but he may be running the risk of narrowing his range of choices and receiving only a limited design service. He may be able to buy an entirely satisfactory service from an experienced producer of packaging.

The techniques of packaging are now so highly developed and the choices so wide that most managers will feel that they need some independent advice before making a final decision. If he has not this expertise with which to reach a decision within his own organisation, then he is well advised to consider using a packaging design consultant, if only on the basic problem of selecting appropriate techniques and the detailed graphics. The manager's main problem may not be technical, but one of persuading higher management that investment in packaging design can be a substantial aid in preserving the character of the product and in promoting those characteristics all along the line of distribution to the point of sale. It is worth taking particular care to set up the design and production of packaging in such a way that some cost-effective analysis can be made afterwards with the marketing division.

The important function of the design of print of all kinds to promote marketing will be dealt with in a later chapter. But whatever the design work the manager will find that the understanding of the basic discipline of the design process will enable him to set requirements, organise the work itself and assess its results. He may, however, have to go through the cycle several times in order to arrive at the optimum solution.

Chapter 2

Design and Marketing

Changes in the market and developments in technology seem to interact on one another so that the rate of change is accelerated. The needs of the market stimulate technological advances which in turn create new needs. The connection between the two is of great interest to the design manager. Management has to look on innovation with a very perceptive eye which will be constantly scanning both technical developments and indications of change in demand from the market so that both can be exploited to give opportunities for growth. It is difficult to cope with this situation in terms of formal organisation; much must depend on the alertness of the managers themselves and the interchange of ideas between technical experts, designers and marketing men.

Design departments need to know as much as possible about the characteristics of new materials and methods of manipulating them in relation to what the market will take. Marketing men and designers may also see a trend which the customer has not fully grasped, but which can be profitably exploited if marketing, design and production can be effectively co-ordinated by management. For example, new materials and machine tools such as plastics and welding techniques can have a great effect on the specification for a shoe. But other developments like air-conditioning and convenience of transport have a pervasive effect on market requirements. The more controlled the environment in the house, the office and the factory and during journeys from A to B the more acceptable is the lightweight shoe in Europe. Awareness is always an important characteristic of a designer and design departments need opportunities to become aware of what is going on in related industries and what needs are arising in the market. This is a problem of communication for management.

Britain has been remarkably successful in producing new ideas from basic research, but has often failed to convert the innovation into marketable hardware by means of skilful design. This is not so much due to a shortage of designers, as to a lack of appreciation by management of how to organise and optimise the activity of designers in relation to marketing and production. Management skills are available and are related to other aspects of an enterprise, but are not sufficiently applied to design work to exploit its full potential. Dr D. Firth at the National Engineering Laboratories, has aptly observed that innovation is a spectrum of activities. At one end is the bold innovating leap and at the other a creeping barrage of minor innovations.

The design manager will be constantly relating designing to marketing and challenging the design team to give physical form to marketing requirements. To do this he needs the backing of a boardroom policy for innovation so that he does not have to battle for design development against a background of inertia. It is understandable that a company nowadays needs to be highly cost-conscious, but it is dangerous if such an attitude, correct though it is in itself, degenerates into a resistance to change by middle management, a resistance which can itself deprive the company of cost benefit achieved through imaginative design. There is always a degree of risk in producing something new but not to do so can diminish a firm's chances in the market. It is also unrealistic to plan on the assumption that 100 per cent of new designs will prove to be market leaders. The plans and the budgets will allow for a small proportion of addled eggs. The design manager, moreover, must be prepared to intervene when he becomes convinced the design development should be chopped because it has become unlikely to succeed in the market due to price, performance or appeal. This is a depressing decision to have to take but it is better than continuing to invest in something which falls short of the essentials in the design brief. No system will eliminate mistakes; the management skill is to recognise them quickly and minimise the consequences.

The rhythm of the design development programme will depend on the estimated life of existing products as well as opportunities for marketing entirely new ones. It is a matter of complex judgement to gear product programmes to market changes. It is however increasingly obvious that the life of many products tends to diminish while their period of design and development increases. The National Marketing Council published a set of simple graphs to show the expected life of a product. The life cycle of the product (horizontal co-ordinate) is plotted against the share of the market (vertical co-ordinate). Section 1 is the period of design development when the market share is nil; Section 2 is the launching period when the product is gaining market acceptance; Section 3 is the period of maturity in the market; and Section 4 is the decline when customers are being lost and will have to be regained by promotion or by a new design programme (figure 8).

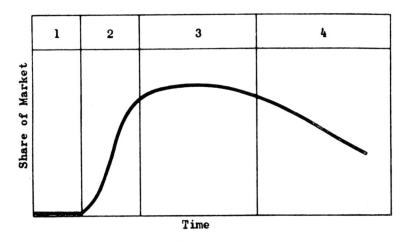

Figure 8

The dilemma for management is to distinguish between temporary fluctuations in the market and the onset of a continual decline. To redesign too early may be an unnecessary diversion of capital resources; to leave it too late runs the risk of losing too many customers who will have to be won back at great expense. Consequently the curves of a product development programme very often look like those in figure 9.

Innovation has become an emergency measure to halt a falling sales graph and not a planned but flexible policy of the company. A few enterprises plan innovation, but most have innovation thrust upon them. In an ideal world the few can look forward to a rising curve along which design work is virtually continuous, but at varying levels of intensity (see figure 10).

New designs are introduced before the rot sets in. Such a state of grace is difficult to achieve, but is none the less an objective to strive for. It will be more likely to be achieved if the design activity in the firm is directed

51

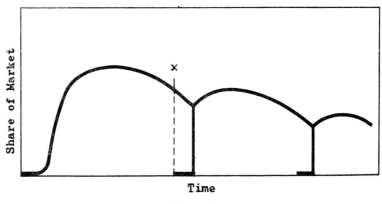

Figure 9

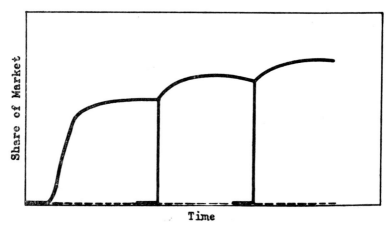

Figure 10

towards customer satisfaction, bearing in mind that this can usually only be done from within the resources of the company. Sophisticated improvements in production can be reflected in additional satisfaction for the customer through price, performance or convenience. The design manager can foster a community of interest between designers and marketing men by concentrating their attention on characteristics which have potential commercial advantage. Friction between design and marketing is a red light for the manager. Design and marketing will tend to have a longer term aim than the sales force.

The design manager will become involved in co-operation with the marketing division, because he has a vital interest in the analysis of the

52

market which is an expert field requiring skilled organisation and practitioners. Using designers is no substitute for them where volume sales are concerned. But accurate and up-to-date market information is essential to designers who will be able to interpret it in the light of their own experience of human behaviour. Their developed intuition will be able to bridge some of the inevitable gaps in the market reports.

Designers can benefit from direct observation of market conditions, not to prepare comprehensive market reports themselves, but to enable them to interpret reports in the most creative manner. Market reports essentially reflect the recent past; the designer and the company itself is equally concerned with the immediate future. Stimulating this imaginative and creative leap forward is an essential part of an aggressive marketing policy. To be too far behind the market can be as disastrous as being too far ahead of it. Research development and production programmes now extend two and three years for quite simple products so the danger of putting on the market something like the bestseller of two years ago which is now beginning to decline is very real.

The assessment of the rate of market changes and the selection of the optimum technical means to meet them is both a managerial task and a design problem. It is the design aspect which is often given less attention by the manager. Perhaps the most difficult situation, commercially and morally, is the long-life product which is sold in a market where customer choice changes rapidly, either by the inducement of publicity or the customer's free will. The automobile is in this category in which there is a very sensitive relationship between selling the basic product and then servicing it. To sell the product, Volkswagen gave the impression of freezing its design, and developed a highly effective servicing network. Here again there is a close relationship between designing the product and managing the service of it. If servicing is a main marketing point then the design of the product must pay particular attention to this.

In consumer goods industries where turnover in models is increasingly rapid, management can regard designing as a more or less continuous process in which new products are brought in to lift the sales graph at the right moment as in the Wilkinson's sales graph, facing p. 96. In the capital goods industries it is a much more complicated calculation to judge at what rate to redesign in order to keep an innovation policy for extending your share of the market continuously. Only by the closest collaboration between marketing, engineering and design can the most

53

profitable decision be reached. A great deal of effort and money usually goes into product development programmes; it is logical that a fair share of that investment should go into design research and designing, because it is through that part of the total activity that the market requirements are turned into saleable hardware.

Management Studies and Design

It is healthy if this reliance on the design activity to create hard selling characteristics in the product, comes substantially from the marketing division, thus avoiding an atmosphere developing of 'design for its own sake'. Basic organisation, staff relationships, and even the positioning of offices can help to prevent this happening. When management considers the internal organisation of the design team for each particular project it is worth giving as much weight to the marketing point of view as to the production and economic aspect. It is, however, necessary to ensure that the designers are given enough elbow room to do the designing. This is often a problem for the manager, because in management training, according to a survey carried out by *Design* magazine, it is rare for there to be any analysis of the particular requirements of design departments. The routine management school attitude is that designing is just like any other activity when it comes to managing it. This can be true up to a point, but as we have seen earlier, the creative aspects of the process need special attention to achieve the best results. This attitude of management teachers derives from the lack of a corpus of documented knowledge and case studies describing the design activity. When the National Marketing Council sent its first team of young business men over to Harvard, I asked several of them to examine some of the famous Harvard case studies and let me know to what extent design was included. The answer was everything else but design. So it is not surprising that some managers feel that designing, like Topsy, just grows up by itself, unnurtured by the hand of management. Experienced management knows that if creativity is not generated at the student and early post-experience stage it is unlikely to manifest itself at all. It is, therefore, all too easy to become lumbered with a completely non-creative design organisation for which management has only itself to blame. Insistence by the marketing division on design innovation can be an effective safeguard against product complacency.

54

User-orientation

Traditionally design departments have been considered as adjuncts to production and this is a sympton of a production-oriented enterprise. Consequently many staff designers become attuned to the production attitude, particularly in the engineering industries, and this can often deflect the direct stimulus which comes from up-to-date and properly sifted market information, indicating what the customer's requirements really are. It is a matter of management organisation to counteract this tendency and to instil into designers and production engineers the mandatory importance of relating the product to market requirements. In some long-established companies the attitude still persists that the correct order of events is for the factory to produce goods in conjunction with the drawing-office and then the salesmen are sent out to create a demand for them. 'We've made it; you sell it.' In such a situation the opportunity for the customer's requirements to be impressed upon the designers is minimal and the marketing prospects are restricted. The customer's reactions to the performance, convenience (including servicing) and the appearance of the product are vital factors in creating the design, and they are factors which the salesmen and advertising agent can use to achieve sales.

If a marketing manager detects that the firm is unduly preoccupied with production problems and that expertise in manufacture is the most highly prized virtue, then he has a challenge before him. Similarly if the attitude to costs is dominated by the accountants to the detriment of selling, rather than an emphasis on value or cost benefit, then product policy may need reviewing from the marketing and design standpoint. The effective interaction between marketing and production is at the core of management's task and neither should be exclusively wagging the tail. Design stands in between, serving both and contributing to the main objectives. Involving designers in conferences of salesmen and marketing managers and exposing them to the experience of service engineers who are in close touch with customers using the product, can promote a dialogue between design and marketing. A marketing manager can exploit the designer's knowledge of human factors, such as ergonomics (the relationship between man and tools) anthropometrics (human dimensions) and environmental influences. The designer's professional training fits him to adopt the stance of the user in appraising the characteristics of the product, rather than relying on the proverbial managing director's wife in consumer goods. This training and attitude can be exploited to the firm's advantage particularly by the marketing division.

Mr H. G. Lazal, as chairman of the Beecham Group, has said that,

. . . in a competitive economy the consumer's convenience is paramount and suppliers have to address themselves to producing what customers want to buy. Marketing is therefore a symptom of a competitive economy and the fiercer the competition, the more important marketing becomes. There must be a willingness to adjust products and, if necessary, organisation and operating methods, to meet the changing needs of customers and the changes in competitive forces. In an age of rapid technological change the public expects improved products and their custom will go to the firms which provide them.

So management has a design problem.

I may have given the impression that the ideal situation is all sweetness and light, a sequence of easy relationships and smooth dialogues between marketing, design and production. This is not so and it would be misleading to the manager to expect it to be. A certain degree of challenge and tension, competition and cut and thrust is essential to the creative stimulus. That is not to say that the designers can only fish in troubled waters, but a creative designer usually indulges in a certain amount of conviction; he is often protective about his brainchild. It is right that this should be challenged by both production and marketing, that the designer should be asked to justify his conviction. But the skilful manager will see to it that this is done constructively and without inflexibility, so that an atmosphere of give and take prevails. Otherwise successful team work becomes impossible. By involving marketing and making a tripartite discussion it is easier to avoid entrenched positions which can so easily lead to deadlock. As a designer, Sir Barnes Wallis was both brilliant and militant, and his contribution to the aircraft industry was enormous.

Market Analysis and Product Planning

It has been said that the art of marketing industrial goods is to know when to stop and ask yourself questions; G. H. Sugden of Simon

Engineering adds 'even mean ruthless questions'. He gives a very good list of questions, concerning the manufacture of flour-milling equipment, which illustrates the breadth and depth of enquiry required in a long-term marketing plan, e.g. changes in population, in consumption of flour *per capita*, in net import/export of flour, in the level of utilisation of existing milling equipment and in the rate it will be replaced and in technical development. He adds the following factors for policy consideration: that world population is expected to double by 2000 A.D.; that consumption of wheat flour *per capita* is increasing in underdeveloped countries, but declining in countries with a high standard of living; that for political reasons emerging nations often build flour mills which may be difficult to justify on economic grounds; that there is a surplus of milling capacity in some parts of the world; that to compensate for the higher cost of plant and buildings, higher capacity machinery has been introduced requiring less space, less supervision and less power to drive it; that vertical integration has led to purchase of bakeries by some large milling groups which is making them more interested in the end product—bread, biscuits or cakes—than the intermediate product flour. Among the key policy questions which this enquiry throws up when it has been quantified and assessed is the design consideration: 'Should we try to develop new processes or equipment which will lengthen the product cycle?' He wisely concludes: 'You will never have all the facts; you must still use your judgements on the facts available. As one of my teachers used to say—you may be no more accurate than the weather forecast, but this will often be enough to give you a head start over your competitors.' The manager's preoccupation is to satisfy himself that forecasts are based upon reliable sources of information.

The basic hazard is not so much the complexity of the factors which are induced by change, but the failure of management to recognise that the market is changing so that a design and development programme can be put in hand sufficiently early in order to benefit from the opportunity offered by change. Consequently the marketing horizon and product planning will be between three and ten years ahead in the heavier industries. This means that a company's product planning group will have a strong bias towards marketing and design, towards investment in those changes which will bring growth quite as much as in the prolongation of the status quo. And the greatest opportunity for growth may lie in the successful designing and marketing of new products.

Mr R. A. Wenham, Managing Director of Motorail, has estimated that although some 90 per cent of new products fail to survive the first two years, certain industries and companies have a high degree of success, many long-established companies having a growing proportion of current sales in products which did not exist ten years ago; that 5 per cent of American industry's growth comes from new products not manufactured ten years ago and new product plans are the heart of growth plans in leading manufacturing companies. The marketing manager today is, therefore, suspicious of the attitude that change should be resisted as long as a product range is selling well. Such a situation is rather a healthy platform for a programme of increasingly successful products whose characteristics will be determined by an imaginative and customer-oriented design department.

One well-tried method of stimulating growth in the market is obsolescence built into the product on the drawing-board. This has attracted some customer resistance. More fundamental and probably more successful in the long run is a product programme which sets out to offer the customer a continual extension of improvement by addition as much as by replacement. Such an attitude depends on a marketing plan to sell a whole system of related products rather than the odd item, but it may be some years before this concept is widely acceptable. It is the same concept that enables a firm to supply a basic range of products to several countries with differing dimensional and safety standards, because the designers have introduced sufficient flexibility into the specification without greatly adding to cost. If designers and marketing men are going to have an effect on attitudes which are over-concerned with production problems, then they have to be able to organise and present their design and marketing research in a form which is not only intelligible to other managers and production engineers but also distinguishes clearly between the facts and the deductions, quantifying information whenever it is possible to do so. Both designers and managers share the basic responsibility to be able to communicate their information and ideas so that the situation becomes simpler and not increasingly confused. Designers particularly should wrestle with the problem of communication because their task is to bring order out of a multitude of miscellaneous factors.

Teamwork

One of the benefits of the closest possible relationships between design and marketing departments is that the chance of fostering separate and confusing jargon is reduced. In-groups tend to generate an in-language which can be a useful shorthand, but it can also be a barrier to wider communication, stultifying the essential exchange of ideas. Technical terms are, of course, necessary, but gobbledegook helps neither manager nor specialist. Assessments of feasibility and reliability cannot be made on the basis of a language only partially understood. However a well-managed team of enthusiastic specialists can soon develop a common understanding; if this does not happen then it is a sure sign that the group is not working as a team through failure to communicate. Communication is important particularly to designers because theirs is the linking activity within a whole series of related activities. A survey of European design departments carried out by the Organisation for Economic Co-operation and Development (Paris 1967) concluded that 'it is all too frequently a fact that the designer does not have the basic information necessary for his work'.

The creation of teams which cut across the formal definition of responsibilities is one of the best ways by which management can facilitate changes in attitude dictated by the market. Through team-work interdepartmental jealousies can be broken down and the shifting of responsibility from one division to another can be smoothly effected. Vested interests can be diluted and the area of decision for the marketing division enlarged, so that it has more influence upon the design of new products. Unfortunately it is very easy for teamwork to degenerate into a proliferation of committees which are no more than talking-shops in which individuals take the opportunity to score points and air grouses so that there is very little exchange of ideas and hardly any progress. I therefore draw some distinction between a committee of high-level executives whose function is to form policy and co-ordinate the broad interests of an enterprise, and a team which has a well-defined problem to solve by means of the several resources commanded by each member. In my view the team which takes on the role of a committee is in real danger of being counter-productive, and endless committee meetings can be both frustrating and stultifying to designers.

The origins of ideas for new products can be very diverse. Certainly a progressive firm needs plenty of suggestions and a high proportion should come from the marketing people if the concept of their job goes further than merely administering a sales force. Most departments are committed, however, to the immediate success of day-to-day operations. There is a danger that no one may be looking beyond the general remit of the product policy group. The design manager on the other hand is in a central position to encourage ideas for new products and to organise their evaluation so that eventually they can be fed into the system of product programming. James Pilditch has described how the formal concept of product planning has been successfully developed by General Electric (USA), Capital Products (USA), Philco and Ekco. He stresses the need for the closest integration with designers, who more than anyone else can ensure that the product is imaginative, always provided that they are brought into the project at an early stage. From his experience there is a direct link between the stage at which the designer is brought in and the value of his contribution. The old idea that the designer is just brought in during the final stages to make the product look pretty dies hard. Product planning is a user-oriented activity and it is concerned with a creative attitude towards the future. Fortunately for industry it is now accepted that future forecasting can be undertaken on a basis of facts, with hunches and guesses reduced to that area of the problem where no precise knowledge exists. Most designers are happier looking forward than peering into the not-so-recent past.

In the composition of project teams it is more important to include the essential interests than to reflect the hierarchical levels of responsibility. Each company will require its own particular mix according to what it is selling and how its products are manufactured; but if marketing is not fully included in product planning then a vital element is missing from the consideration of the design brief. In the early stages of planning a product a great deal of analysis has to be carried out (see chapter 1), but this should not exclude as much creative thinking as management can stimulate. As a preliminary to this the technique of brainstorming can be fruitful, using a group of up to a dozen people, chosen from widely different disciplines. Marketing people are valuable participants in the group because their minds are usually alert to a wide range of possibilities, and they also have direct experience of the users' reactions to the product; nor are they hedged about by a multitude of narrow technical problems. In brainstorming it is important that the manager should not only have this wide range of interests but that each member should feel free, indeed obliged, to throw out each idea that comes into his or her head without reflection. There must also be an absolute understanding that no contribution will be laughed out of court. Such reactions immediately create an atmosphere of selfconsciousness and inhibit the flow of ideas.

A typical brainstorming group might include production engineering, design, sales and marketing (including export), product testing, buying, library services, research and accounting. This gives a balance between the inward-looking services of production, cost accounting and product testing and the outward-looking services of design, marketing and research. The manager's role is to stimulate the spontaneous and random discussion and to make sure that worthwhile contributions do not vanish into thin air as one unorthodox suggestion follows another. Each participant may also discover a great deal about his colleagues' knowledge and experience which hitherto had never been discussed. Even if the ideas which emerge have little practical value, each one taking part may end up with a much greater awareness of the total pool of knowledge available to solve the problem. Such sessions are all the better if they are not held too frequently and are conducted at a brisk tempo for a comparatively short time, say one-and-a-half hours, rather than drag on for half a day. It will usually take about twenty minutes to warm up, followed by about eighty minutes of quick-firing dialogue. The manager will find that the pace will depend much on the degree of enthusiasm and encouragement that he can personally contribute to the session, which can be regarded as an antidote to long periods of intensive analysis which must remain the backbone of planning products for a carefully defined market. Brainstorming can be truly exhausting so it is well to time the end to coincide with the lunch break or the end of the day. The manager will be surprised how much of value comes during a jam-session from the sales and marketing end of the spectrum.

Sir William Mather has observed in his own engineering firm that, 'the customer can be and often is, the best stimulant to design . . . he can help to solve problems and improve production methods'. Therefore, the people who are in constant touch with customers can make a valuable contribution to the design of a company's product. If they cannot, then the manager will start asking why not. Experience in export markets particularly can provide a new assessment of a product or a service, which may improve the prospects in the home market. The main concern of brainstorming will always be to get the blinkers off and have an entirely new look at the situation, because it is very easy to have a policy of innovation and to pay lip-service to it, but in fact be bankrupt of new ideas. Having held a session the manager will make sure that there is some feedback which shows that something of value has emerged, otherwise those involved will become rather cynical about management's innovation policy. The objective must be clear at the start, and the extent to which it has been reached declared at the end. Tracing results is not always easy and this makes the attempt all the more necessary.

Design and Selling

There are widely differing opinions about the extent to which salesmen should be brought into the design process. Some firms with much experience believe that the salesman need not be brought in until the product is designed and about to be launched. Others believe quite as strongly that the sales point of view must be heard from the beginning. Those who adopt the attitude of excluding the salesmen are apprehensive that the sales force will put the brake on innovation, that they will only encourage minor modifications which will make the product more like its best-selling competitor and will oppose any major advance by saying it won't sell. I would hope, however, that this type of salesman is on the decrease, because they are alien to the dynamic sort of sales force which is needed in competitive markets today. The opposite point of view has been well put by Sir Roger Falk:

> I have seen from the receiving end the reaction of salesmen in the field to a Head Office circular telling him of the necessity to go out and sell a newly designed product about which he had previously heard nothing. This is bad business. Apart from the fact that salesmen can often contribute valuable market comment and criticism in the planning stage, the imposing of new designs on a sales force without prior briefing with a fully explained 'reason why' session with top management makes for dissatisfaction and discontent.

Obviously every salesman should know exactly why a product has been designed with particular characteristics so that he can explain convincingly to the prospective customer. Moreover, if his department has been concerned with the design and development of the product the salesman will become identified with it and committed to its eventual success in the market. It will be his product as much as anybody else's. Even if the firm attributes the design to a designer with a famous name, then the salesman can feel that he has a personal relationship with him if management has arranged for the designer to give a briefing session to the sales force. If salesmen are constantly left out of the design development, it is not surprising that they become a little resentful of new designs, and address themselves to the more conservative elements in the market. Salesmen are by the nature of their job vitally interested in the firm's products and proud of their merits. One way in which management can achieve this is by identifying salesmen with design development.

There are practical ways in which this can be done. Most design briefs contain some data which can be effectively used in selling. An office chair, for example, may have been designed with particular attention to reduction of fatigue in the office worker. The height of the seat may have reduced substantially the obstruction which its front edge can cause to circulation in the legs. The configuration of the back may give good support to the lumbar region when working at a desk. Its covering may be particularly easy to change for cleaning. It is one thing to say to a customer 'see how comfortable it is' and another to be able to explain what design characteristics make a chair comfortable. To a customer evidence of painstaking design provides some tangible evidence that the product will prove satisfactory. This is much more convincing sales talk than a string of vague clichés which constitute much of the patter directed towards customers. Equally, however good the patter, regular customers are unlikely to be won if the design of a product is wrong. The salesman or the service engineer may be the one person who knows from first-hand experience why it is wrong. When a product does not sell it is natural to examine closely the marketing plan and the performance of the sales force but even a perfect textbook marketing operation will not overcome basic faults in the design of a product. Salesmen need training in the science of selling and also in the appraisal of products. In selling machine tools it is no longer sufficient to assure the customer that it will do its job in a narrow sense, and that it is robust with nothing less than two inches thick; it is equally necessary to show that convenience in use, ease of maintenance, and safety have been designed into the product. A salesman needs to know in general terms how this has been done.

At this point it is perhaps worth making a distinction between marketing and sales. Mr P. J. Natsler, managing director of A.R.O. Machinery Company Limited, says that his firm defines a sales manager as dealing with people and a marketing manager as dealing with figures and graphs. This is oversimplified but touches upon the essentials; it also shows why it is easier to involve marketing men in product planning whilst the sales manager as such is often left out. Rightly the sales manager is out on the job and the marketing manager is conveniently to hand in his office. But if a sales manager is ineffective when he is not out in constant touch with the customer, by the same token the marketing manager is ineffective if he is only in remote contact with the sales force. Communications is the essence of management and particularly so in the case of design management which should be a central activity at the core of the company's operations. The salesman may be one stage removed from the design activity but he should not be divorced from it.

Where new products have been planned on the basis that they are meeting a growth market, then it is reasonable for management to expect that growth will be gradually reflected in the order books of the salesmen. If, however, the salesman who actually confronts the customer has had inadequate training in the product's history, then the growth may be slow. New products are always a challenge to the sales force and often involve approaches to a new type of customer. Familiarity with the design story can stimulate the customer's interest in a new range. Although every buyer is ostensibly open to something new the introduction of a new line successfully requires considerable skill. Not every well-designed product reveals its merits at a first glance. In fact its very strangeness may be both a disadvantage as well as an advantage. If the salesman can quote recognition of new products by independent authorities such as the Consumers' Association's *Which?* and the black and white label of the Design Council these are useful shots in the locker. The designer's contribution can be reflected in almost every aspect. As the designer Kenneth Grange put it: 'I have a clear vision of every product as a fine, beautiful thing, fit for its purpose, a pleasure to own, handle and use, a compliment to the user and a bargain for the purchaser.' If every designer lived up to this promise the salesman's lot would be a good deal easier.

A design manager does not expect that the salesman will have the ability to assess how a product will finally be from preliminary sketches and crude prototypes. I believe that the reason why some firms mistrust the reaction of salesmen to new ideas is that proposals are shown to them in a form which does not enable them to make a realistic judgement. For this reason some textile producers will not show new designs to salesmen until they are actually in cloth. The important aspect for management is that sales staff must be carried with the design development and their co-operation ensured. Without their enthusiastic support few designs are likely to succeed. Once again the essential element is contact and communication with the product planners, detailed explanation being carefully given so that salesmen are fully and effectively briefed about new products. This means avoiding disappointment because an idea has been put across before sufficient detail is available to satisfy the practical standpoint of the salesman, and equally avoiding a breakdown in communication so that they feel they have been left out of the planning and only brought in at the final stage when the product has to be sold.

In marketing, as in most other activities, there is always the intangible but dynamic effect of leadership. As techniques of market research improve and forecasting becomes increasingly more exact, so competing firms share a greater knowledge of what the market demand is. In such a situation there is great commercial advantage for the firm whose design developments succeed in diverting public acceptance into new channels. It is difficult to achieve and even when successful the speed of communication makes the advantage short-lived unless production, distribution and promotion are skilfully co-ordinated. To shrink from the difficulty, however, is probably an unwise policy and to aim at leadership in some degree is the best hope of survival. Having chosen to lead, a great responsibility devolves on the sales force to win a large enough share of the market for new ranges of products. Only a highly trained sales team, enthusiastic about innovation, is likely to be equal to the challenge. Courses of design appreciation for salesmen are a main plank of effective selling of new products; this training itself gives a sense of participation in the creation of the products. To the design manager courses for a salesman are a part of a product development programme.

Presentation: *Print*

Marketing men and designers are both sensitive to the emotional impact of the product on the customer and the manner of its presentation to the customer. On the other hand, the difference in their training and experience may cause them to have very different views about it. The manager will aim to establish some common ground between them. In general the marketing man will have the wider experience of actual point-of-sale reactions to products; the designer will have a greater training in human factors and behavioural patterns. Every sales promotion plan requires close co-operation between marketing and design services in order to achieve maximum impact upon distributor and customer. This impact depends on the successful presentation of the product's characteristics through the promotion media, the principal of which is usually print. Consequently the manager needs to know how to co-ordinate the various specialists who are involved in print and its ancillary service of exhibition. The main consideration for the manager is that print, exhibitions, point-of-sale material, TV advertising and all the facilities of mass media, are a means to an end and not an end in themselves. Typographers are concerned with clear and effective type, photographers with eye-catching and illuminating pictures, exhibition designers with attractive and compelling displays. The manager's constant concern is that these services are directed towards profitable results. Sales are usually the most important of these objectives.

The first priority for the manager is the content of the message, and this must be thoroughly sorted out before the various services of presentation start work, The stage of defining the content is the one which is most often skimped in favour of exploiting the design services which can present the product. As content is more tangible in the medium of print, it is usually convenient to describe first the contribution which print will make to the sales promotion plan. *Design* magazine commissioned Mr Alec Davis to examine the organisation of print for selling in world markets. In a supplement he set out a compendium of useful advice which included a valuable check-list, 'What designers need to know'. This check-list summarises the questions which a manager must answer before organising the design services for print. Its logic follows the same form as has already been recommended for briefing the design team for a product, and it is of particular interest to managers whose firms provide services rather than products, because the promotion of services such as banking, insurance, dry cleaning or travel depends so much on the effective designing of print.

Mr Davis's check-list helps the manager to clear his own mind about the job and the answers to it provide the basis for briefing the design services which are required. It reads thus:

The designer must have a comprehensive brief if his skills are to be used to their best advantage. Such a brief cannot be formulated until the manufacturer has himself analysed the project and has a clear idea of its purpose and of the people at whom it is directed. The check-list below has been devised to help the manufacturer clarify his own thoughts as well as to provide information that will be essential for the designer. The answers to these questions will to some extent be instructions to the designer; but they will also be a basis for discussion between him and his client.

Two important points for the manufacturer to bear in mind are: first, that the brief should clearly set out in writing the information the designer and printer will need at all stages of the job; and second, that the person appointed by the company to brief the designer, and to follow the job's progress through to completion, should be able to make decisions which will not be overruled.

CHECK-LIST

1 Purpose and nature of the job
   (*a*) Is it to advertise your products (e.g. leaflets, display material)?
        To instruct people in their use, installation or maintenance (e.g. instruction leaflets, handbooks, wording on packs)?
        To protect and/or contain them (e.g. packaging)?
        To provide specific information about them (e.g. catalogues, descriptive booklets)?
        To remind people of your company's name, or give general information about its activities (e.g. house organs, prestige booklets, letter-headings)?
   (*b*) Is it a new job, an adaptation of an existing one, an isolated item, or part of a range?
   (*c*) Is one piece of print intended to serve too many purposes?

Would two simpler items, each having a separate purpose, be more satisfactory?

2 Coverage
   (a) For whom is it intended—housewives? teenagers? technical experts? Trade or professional groups? People with sophisticated tastes?
   (b) In which countries overseas?

3 Copy
   (a) What information is required, and in what sequence?
   (b) What are regarded as the chief selling points? Will they be affected by differences in national preferences or requirements?
   (c) Are there any special statutory or other legal requirements in particular countries?
   (d) Are overseas agents' names to be printed? Or is space to be allowed for these to be locally overprinted or stamped?
   (e) Are prices to be included? On a separate list or as part of the job?
   (f) Is inclusion of an SfB reference number appropriate?

4 Languages
   (a) Is the job to be printed in English only? In English plus foreign languages? In foreign languages only? In English with foreign language summaries? In English first, with illustrations then 'run on' for later substitution of foreign languages in further copies?
   (b) If in foreign languages, which ones?
   (c) Will there be a separate edition for each language? Or one multi-lingual edition?
   (d) Will the necessary translations be supplied? Or is the designer asked to recommend a translator?
   (e) When copy is received, will this be final? Or will overseas vetting of the typsecript still be required? Will this be done—as it should be—at proof stage?

5 Style
   (a) Is it the British character of your products that counts most abroad?

(*b*) Or do you wish to be known for your awareness of international trends?

(*c*) Or are you more concerned with the appropriateness of your product to a particular market?

(*d*) Should the design conform to an existing house style?

(*e*) If not, does this mean that a new house style is needed?

6 Illustrations

(*a*) Are you providing photographs or drawings that are essential?

(*b*) Are there existing illustrations that are optional?

(*c*) If new illustrations are required, are they to be provided by you or by the designer? If by the designer, is he to quote for these separately from the basic design fee?

(*d*) Are there any other sources of suitable illustrations (e.g. photographic libraries, agencies)?

(*e*) Are enough illustrations being used to minimise language difficulties?

7 Sizes

(*a*) Should the job be in A4, A5 or another A size?

(*b*) Or should it be in US quarto (11 × 8½ inches) or some subdivision of this?

(*c*) Or in any other size, either laid down by you or suggested by the designer?

8 Production

(*a*) What quantities are required?

(*b*) What kind and quality of paper, board and/or other materials are to be used?

(*c*) Is the designer free to select the printing method—e.g. letterpress, lithography, gravure, screen process or a combination of two or more of these?

(*d*) Is the designer required to recommend a printer or to use your regular printer?

(*e*) If the designer recommends a printer, is he to obtain competitive quotations?

(*f*) If your own printer is used, is he experienced in foreign language printing?

(g) What are the time limits for design, printer's proofs, and delivery of the completed job? (These schedules must be more extended than for home market printing if the translation is to be sound and the checking competent.)

(h) Are copies to be dispatched overseas by the printer? Or sent to you for individual mailing to overseas addresses? Or to you for bulk shipment overseas? Or to some other address for bulk shipment?

The answers to these questions will not only define the printing job, it will also show the kind of specialists required such as technical and copy writers for text, artists and photographers (possibly models) or illustrators, translators, typographers, printers, proof-readers and distributors. Inexperienced managers are apt to think that printed material just happens and this attitude invariably causes delay, frustration, unnecessary expense, as well as inaccurate and unsatisfactory work. Much of this can be avoided if the manager has a clear idea of the purpose the print will serve, the readers at whom it is directed and the services needed to produce it. The special problems of packaging have already been discussed in relation to the production of the product because it follows logically at that stage. Many of the decisions concerning print are similar.

The work can be put through the firm's advertising agent who will have the appropriate specialists and who will co-ordinate them. The manager's responsibility then is to make his requirements absolutely clear to the account executive and decide whether the work subsequently submitted meets them. Alternatively he can select a graphic designer who will act as an independent consultant, submitting finished artwork and typographical instructions for the printer. Normally only large concerns have sufficient printing work to justify the overheads of their own production department for print, artwork and photography. Most will have an advertising agent, but the manager may decide that he can best get what he wants by working directly with his own consultant graphic designer who can give the job an individual character which will conform with the firm's graphic style (see chapter 4). In that case responsibilities must be carefully defined.

Text

The manager will certainly be responsible for most of the text and he will run into trouble if he himself does not produce a professional job. Designers are often confronted with a half-baked text, sloppily written, prolix, illogically constructed, ambiguous and even contradictory. The point has already been made that a design manager must be a skilled communicator and able to précis. Preparing text for print is one of his testing times, and more often than not causes much anguish and despair. To persuade colleagues to give him accurate and complete information and then to express it in a form which will satisfy all members of the Board and the customer is a rare achievement. The permanency of the final printing of a leaflet brooks no second thoughts. The manager has the unenviable task of making sure that the text which reaches the designer is the final one. Rewriting at proof stage can be both exasperating and expensive; it can destroy the whole layout of a page and cause a chain reaction of dislocation throughout a whole publication.

It is a common fault to underestimate the time it takes to prepare, agree on, edit and check even the simplest texts. The essential information has to be isolated and then written up. Many departments are involved and the text usually is a hotchpotch. Skilful editing then puts it into shape and the result has to be agreed by the experts involved. In no time the exercise can become a ball of wool if the manager is not perspicacious, vigilant and patient. Inevitably the timetable is in danger, but the manager must at all cost resist the temptation to pass on unresolved text to the graphic designer or the advertising agent, because they are unlikely to succeed at second hand where he has failed. By hook or by crook, by stealth, guile or low cunning he must achieve a satisfactory agreed text before the job is put in hand. This applies mainly to leaflets, handbooks, catalogues, letter headings, reports, and instruction manuals. Advertising copy is best handled by the professionals in the agency and good results are achieved by a subtle and creative relationship in which successful agencies are highly skilled.

The manager is half-way home when he succeeds in finalising a text which his colleagues really do recognise as final. This includes obtaining the approval of agents and overseas agents to wording and translations. Generally translations are of a poor standard and too often no translation is attempted at all. The manager has to find out what translations are essential to successful marketing and then make sure that they are done accurately in appropriate and up-to-date phrasing. Help in finding competent translators can be obtained from the Institute of Linguists, from the Association of Special Libraries and Information Bureaux and from the information staff of your embassy in the country with which you are concerned. It pays to be suspicious of translators who are purely academic or who have been out of touch with the country concerned for some years. If a text has to be translated into foreign languages it is always best to aim at a simple and direct style in the original. Mr Davis refers to the Dutch bulb-grower who promoted his product in England as 'amazing bloomers'. If a leaflet is to be printed in several languages, rather than a separate version for each, there are special problems because English takes up less space than most other languages, due to its rich vocabulary. The layout must be designed to allow for this, so that the result is not ragged.

With these textual problems solved, matters of size, delivery dates, methods of dispatch, quantity, paper, illustrations (previously agreed with the experts), colour and cost can be worked out with the designer and the printer. Dates for galleys, page and final proofs can be fixed. It is a matter of judgement whether proofs should be submitted to those who have contributed to the text. Admittedly most of them will have itchy pencils and will start having second thoughts and rewriting. If the manager feels that accuracy is best served by doing so, he can minimise thoughtless alterations by attaching to the proof a copy of the typescript originally agreed by the author. This has a curbing effect on feckless contributors. One further point is important; corrections on the proof returned to the printer must be in recognised printers' symbols and should, therefore, be done by the designer. Sufficient proofs must be ordered in the first place to allow for circulation and a final marked-up copy for the printer.

ILLUSTRATIONS

Effective illustrations are a powerful aid to selling even highly technical products. Unfortunately most illustrations lack punch and point; they are too generalised to contribute much to the message. A rough rule is that an illustration should either inform or attract attention, preferably both. If it does neither then it is probably a waste of time. It should also if possible save some textual space. Briefing a photographer is a skilled

72

business, but most graphic designers are accustomed to this and so are art directors in advertising agencies. Photography can be expensive so it is worth thrashing out thoroughly exactly what point requires illustration before involving the photographer. Endless series of photographs on a trial-and-error basis can be expensive, and the contract with the photographer should be carefully drawn to describe the method of working. A roll of film is not expensive but if you are paying by the shot the cost can rise steeply. Carefully prepared instructions can provide the basis for many exposures in a reasonably short space of time in a manner

Figure 11

satisfactory both to client and photographer. This is not an area in which the manager should attempt to economise by acting himself as the art director.

An alternative to photographs is line drawings which can be more explicit than photographs, particularly in presenting technical information, if they are as well drawn as figure 11. In describing consumer goods drawings can also introduce a touch of humour, although this must be handled with discretion. The snag is that skilful illustrators are very hard to find and they are expensive. Line blocks, however, are slightly cheaper than half-tones and much cheaper than colour blocks. If a first-rate illustrator cannot be found it is better to concentrate on an effective photograph.

QUANTITIES AND QUALITY

Accurate calculations of quantities required can also save money because the cost of running on the machines once the copy is set up is not great, whereas it is more expensive to put it back on the machines again and make ready for a second running. It is always difficult to be accurate about sales literature, but it is worth making a serious examination of the distribution required and the expected life of the piece of print, in order to make the quantity as accurate as possible. Slap-dash guesswork usually results either in a panic reprint or a pulping of surplus stock. If in doubt err on the generous side. Lack of sales literature is likely to be more harmful to the enterprise than a surplus.

Printing is a highly competitive business and time must be allowed for taking estimates from reliable firms. Printers do not like to refuse work, so when they are very busy they often put a substantial price on a job to put a brake on incoming orders. A high price does not necessarily mean that you will receive special attention and a high quality result. It may mean that the printer has too many jobs on hand and that yours is an embarrassment which may get short shrift or even be subcontracted. Similarly a low price may mean that the printer is slack and has time to give careful attention to your work. Both graphic designers and advertising agents are familiar with these situations and should protect you from getting your eggs in the wrong basket. Some printers have excellent design services which are often costed as part of the overheads; such firms can be a great help to the young manager who is feeling his way.

74

Supervising print requires special concentration and attention to detail which the busy manager cannot be expected to do himself. His job is to put the work in competent hands when accurate requirements have been stated and then ensure that the result fits the specification. He should make sure that the person looking after it has the right technical knowledge, an eagle eye for detail and a proven ability to chase work, keep to timetables without making enemies and above all not become neurotic or ill when target dates are threatened as they so often are in the world of print.

The effort is thoroughly worth while because well-designed print of high quality can be a powerful force of silent salesmen in a marketing programme. It is also an outward and visible sign of the quality standards of a firm. A rag-bag of print often indicates a lack of managerial control and insensibility to marketing requirements. An experienced graphic designer can, with very limited means, create a highly favourable impression of a firm's standing. For the manager good print can be the spring-board for the development of a penetrating design policy which will ultimately affect the whole personality of an organisation. To prove the value of print in the area of marketing is an effective way of establishing the cost-effectiveness of design work.

Exhibitions

Exhibitions are a very specialised form of promotion in which there has been some disenchantment during the last decade, largely because it is often difficult to evaluate what they achieve. Certainly the generalised exhibit presented to an amorphous public has latterly run into much criticism. Exhibitions are, however, a form of promotion which should be considered, but not automatically accepted as part of a promotion programme. Exhibiting can easily become an automatic tradition within an organisation long after its original justification has disappeared. The cost of exhibiting, moreover, has risen steeply and other methods of promotion have developed as alternatives. So the manager can approach proposals for an exhibition programme with a wary eye, particularly when they originate from those to whom exhibitions are their lifeblood. From the managerial point of view it is sound practice to make sure that money for exhibitions has constantly to compete with the demands for other kinds of promotion. This ensures a regular assessment of the cost-effectiveness of exhibitions and prevents the automatic provision for

75

participation in some annual event. Large firms may have a need to participate in some of the vast generalised exhibitions for reasons of prestige or broad impact on a market. This can be particularly appropriate if an entirely new range of merchandise is being launched. Very small firms also may rely on general exhibitions such as the Frankfurt Fair to fill a large slice of their order books once or twice a year. Cost can be kept down while a small firm makes itself known and attracts regular visits from buyers. As the firm grows other media may prove more rewarding.

The type of exhibition which the manager will have to consider carefully is the specialised event which draws internationally exactly the buyer in whom he is interested. If the majority of his competitors take part then there will be compelling reasons why his firm should be there. If the firm has not exhibited before in such an annual exhibition, it is reasonable to plan to take part on a three-year trial basis. An assessment after only one year, unless overwhelmingly obvious, is unlikely to be reliable. Having established that a particular exhibition is attended by sufficient buyers who would be potentially interested in the goods being marketed, the manager can start to plan. An exhibition as part of a marketing plan will be a useful link with the customer and this will be the primary aim. But an imaginative exhibition designer can also make it a spring-board for editorial publicity which is often hard to get for a commercial enterprise.

CONTROL

Exhibiting is highly competitive and it is hardly worth being an also-ran. So the selection of the exhibition team is more important than a large budget, although even the most creative designers can be frustrated by too tight a purse. As with print there are two main aspects, content and presentation. An exhibition is a blunt weapon and it cannot be expected to convey a wealth of information. A few essential points for display should be selected and put across clearly and dramatically. If the manager finds himself commissioning a wordy exhibition, he has probably chosen the wrong medium. From a clear statement of objective a theme can be developed in simple direct visual terms. A competent script writer is an essential part of most exhibitions which aim to do more than just put products on pedestals. This is a vital job even though the final result may only be a score of short sentences. Round this the presentation is devised by the display designer who will need graphic and lighting services as well as carpenters and exhibition assistants. Only a few firms have such extensive exhibition programmes that they require their own exhibition department; most put the work out to an exhibition contractor. In order to get the best out of the contractor it is normally wise to use a consultant exhibition designer who can work out a detailed plan well in advance, commission the auxiliary services and then supervise the erection which has to be done in the very short period when the exhibition hall is available for mounting the exhibits. Contractors do have design services, but in this competitive field where creative imagination is at a premium and the plan has to be executed under such exacting conditions, it is well worth having your own consultant designer, whose whole effort will be concentrated on gaining maximum impact for your exhibit and controlling the costs within the agreed budget.

It is not easy for the manager to foresee what he is getting for his money during the planning stage, so he must choose well when he appoints his designer. He can then encourage an enterprising and fresh approach to the display and make sure that all the information and material which the firm has to supply is there on time. Delay can be disastrous, forcing up the cost at the last minute and advertising the firm's inefficiency to the public. It is also a great temptation to interfere in the final stages of the preparation of the display, as fears develop that it is not going to turn out well. Intervention by the layman can cause chaos and should only be allowed if you are absolutely certain that something has gone wrong. There is an element of theatre in exhibitions and the old conviction that it will be all right on the night has its virtue in display work. If it turns out otherwise, sack your designer and have another dip in the bag next time. But it is not in your interest to shoot the pianist until the concert is over.

Exhibition design is quite different from product design. It is a much more exuberant art. It can include familiar symbols, but it must always be fresh and stimulating. The manager will always be on the watch for the first hint of staleness and a tendency towards unimaginative repetition. These are the signs that a change of design leadership is needed. It is a field in which the manager can be venturesome, trying out younger talent and experimenting. It is a nerve-racking responsibility but it should be stimulating; if it is not, the results are probably dull and less

77

effective than they could be. On the other hand, it needs tight budgetary control; wastage can be high in time and material; shortage of time is often the excuse for a last-minute burst of unexpected expenditure. Faced with a deadline in a few hours' time, the manager has not much choice, but if it becomes a habit then the team needs reshuffling. In all exhibition work the manager is poised like the impresario between the imaginative spendthrift and the tight-lipped accountant. He should never let the latter get on top, nor the former bankrupt him. Balance is all in the display game, and a reasonable margin for contingencies under the manager's personal control will ease a lot of headaches. The designer is the key man, obtaining the tenders and estimates within the agreed budget and maintaining day-to-day control of the expenditure. He cannot be ridden on too tight a rein because he must have some flexibility and opportunity to improvise. The best solution is a close working relationship with management.

PUBLICITY

To make an exhibition successful all the publicity stops need to be pulled out, a carefully devised mailing list of invitations, a VIP list for the opening day with a photographer to hand, press releases in advance and handouts and photographs available for the press (a case of gin always helps but it is no substitute for hard information and pictures which the journalist can actually use). An event half-way through the run of the exhibition to give the publicity a lift is a help, a distinguished visitor or a statement about an exceptional order. The main point is that an exhibition should not be unveiled and left to look after itself. It needs energetic promotion designed to declare emphatically the identity of the firm which otherwise may be lost in the general mêlée.

The frantic competition of the large exhibition hall and the doubtful standards of quality which prevail in some of them has led some firms to hold their own separate exhibition in a neighbouring hotel at the same time when all the visiting buyers are available. This breakaway approach requires a different design and promotion technique to achieve a more intimate and exclusive environment akin to a showroom. It is much less complicated as an exhibition problem, but it does require sufficient space to allow staff to discuss business in comfort with visitors when they arrive one after the other. A hole-in-the-corner atmosphere is embarrassing. Before deciding to exhibit in this manner, it is important to make sure that the premises are suitable, the necessary services available, particularly lighting and basic catering facilities, with access for materials when mounting the exhibit and access for visitors throughout your opening hours. The more direct the access from the main entrance usually the better. The talent required for designing this type of exhibit is a mixture between exhibition design and interior design and it is not difficult to find the two combined in the same consultant designer. However good the exhibit is, success depends on a first-rate mailing list and an attractively designed invitation card giving exact details concerning how to find the place. The atmosphere should contrive to create an impression of a reception, even if it goes on for several days, and visitors may expect to meet some senior management whatever time they call. So the running of this kind of exhibit is more complex in terms of stage management, staff attendance, catering arrangements and public relations. If trade visitors get the impression that they have arrived too late at a party which has just finished, it will be counter-productive. Success depends on a subtle blend of design presentation and good housekeeping, Thus it creates an opportunity for some of the administrative staff to be involved in an external activity.

REGULATIONS

Most exhibition sites are governed by a strict set of regulations and also local authority by-laws, particularly about access, fire and loadings. These tend to run to a similar pattern from site to site. They are the direct concern of the designer, but the manager may find it useful to build up a check-list so that he can quickly satisfy himself that there will not be a last-minute crisis because some regulation has been overlooked. Fire inspectors particularly can be most intractable. Miss Dorothy Goslett has a reliable list of standard clauses in her book *The Professional Practice of Design* which is written from the designer's point of view. Clearly exhibitions, like print, are demanding undertakings. The production of print in any diversity requires a supervisor who is constantly checking and chasing. It should not be so, but in nearly all cases it turns out to be necessary. The same is true of exhibitions and most managers will want a capable, if part-time, progress assistant who will keep tabs on the exhibition programme. The alternative is to hand over the whole job to one of the large exhibition contractors who will doubtless produce a reliable job on time. But exhibition work needs fire in its belly and if the digestive tract is too long the fire is apt to go out.

Prospects for Design Managers

Whereas the management of design for production can be reduced to a large extent to methodology and defined procedures combined with an ability to stimulate and co-ordinate, the management of design services to support marketing is a much less exact discipline. It requires a more flexible and opportunist attitude on the part of the manager, and demands a different kind of flair in the design team. On the whole product design teams are different animals from exhibition or print design teams. All require professional training, developed intelligence, intuition and ability to control budgets. But the experience needed and the mixture of the talents is different and the manager will recognise this and compose his teams for the different jobs accordingly. If his own organisation is not of the monolithic structural type, but is flexible and capable of being project-oriented, the manager finds it easier to integrate the management of design teams with the philosophy of his firm.

The design manager may in fact find himself becoming an innovator in the management style of his own company. His insistence on the definition of objectives, his formulation of design briefs, his organisation of projects by teams, his use of group discussion to achieve an integrated course of action, rather than lowest denominator compromise or a 'victor and defeated' situation, his use of conflict as a constructive rather than a negative element in group interaction, and his creation of opportunities to demonstrate talent and to achieve job satisfaction, all have relevance to the development of modern management. So the design manager need not feel that he is in a dead-end job. He has ample opportunity to demonstrate that he is ripe for promotion. In devoting his talents as much to effectiveness of marketing as of production, he is running with the tide of management philosophy. In managing design he will not have to resort to management by exception; he will find that much of his business school training will apply. But he does need to be familiar with the nature of the design process and this in turn may teach him something about the management of people other than designers, their creative abilities and the satisfactions they seek.

Overspecialisation has been the undoing of many species. The wide scope and synthetic character of design management should ensure a firm foot on the promotion ladder, because the experience gained in design work is not much available in management training. He will moreover have no fear of change because he will have learnt to manage it.

Chapter 3

Dealing with Designers

The first step towards getting the best out of designers is to understand how they are trained. This is the clue to the nature of the raw material and how its potential is developed. Experienced designers come in two sizes, staff designers and consultants, and the manager will probably have to deal with both. The basic training for each may be the same, but the management of their several activities differs. Either can come from one of two main sources: the technical colleges (thence for a few to the university) which produce a stream of competent engineers and technicians, some of whom spin off into design careers; and the art schools in which many designers for the consumer goods industries are educated to a national design qualification. The majority of designers who originate in the technical colleges use their engineering skills to become staff designers in the engineering industry. Likewise many designers from art colleges employ their design qualifications in staff design offices, although as a proportion rather more of the art school output become freelance designers. It is helpful for the manager to know the strengths and shortcomings in each group so that he can exploit and supplement accordingly. The greatest mistake is to imagine that the candidate from either school is turned out as a fully competent practitioner. That is just not possible in a complex and creative discipline like design. Firms which constantly complain that this should be so have not come to grips with the nature of the design activity and consequently are likely to have constant trouble in staff design offices, with a high rate of staff turnover or a low output of creative solutions. Some form of internal training is essential even in smaller firms and must be planned and budgeted for.

82

Education: *Technical Colleges*

The technical colleges provide a generally satisfactory syllabus in engineering subjects on which various levels of formal qualification are then based. Engineering principles will have been adequately covered by the study of movement and forces, the technology of construction and manufacturing methods, but more experience will be needed in workshop practice and particular attention will still have to be paid to the stimulation of creative design work. This design training is the most difficult aspect to cover in internal schemes because in theory it is best done in the late teens in a laboratory atmosphere of a college or research establishment. On the other hand, creative stimulus derives from contact with other creative minds which are not always to be found in colleges. So management has to regard this vital aspect as a joint college/industry responsibility and work out a method of dealing with it partly in the college and partly in the works. The first essential is close contact between the two and this is not often as realistic and as continuous as it should be. The design manager can take the initiative to establish an effective liaison, if it does not exist already, with the local technical college or, if more appropriate to his industry, the local art college. He will be welcome because he will be regarded as a useful source of jobs for qualified ex-students. This contact can then be reinforced at the policy level by persuading one of the younger directors to take an interest in the management of the college, so that emphasis can be put on the practical and creative aspects of the engineering syllabus. In most cases the college will need help in the development of design instruction. It is a subject about which ideas are changing rapidly in professional practice and the teaching of fifteen years ago is inadequate for present requirements. Also it is not yet possible to mug up the subject in books. Industry has to be prepared to release some of its first-rate designers to colleges in order that suitable design education can be undertaken. This is happening at university level, but the enlightened firm will see the distinct advantages of doing this at the local college also. Inconveniently it is the experienced young designer, whom the head of department says cannot be spared, who is the right man to release for this task. The design manager will now have enough foresight to solve that problem, because he can argue that contact with the young minds which are potentially at their most creative can also benefit

83

the more experienced designer. The gain is not only an improved output from the college but also greater creative stimulus to the staff man. This channel of practical experience between college and industry cannot be underrated and industry is cutting off its own nose if it neglects it. Release and sandwich methods are common in many trades and have proved worth while despite the difficulties.

Within the factory training is also necessary to develop the recruit from the college to the point where his design performance begins to reward the company. Here again there is advantage in close contact with the teaching staff of the college who can contribute to effective methods of training within the factory. The attitude of industry to colleges of 'you train them, we'll use them', is fast becoming out of date, and the training function within industry is being recognised. The manager's problem is to extend this function to include the less understood activity of design. He will probably find that his concern will widen from design training for designers to design appreciation courses for salesmen and production engineers. The Design Council has much experience in the running of design appreciation courses and its assistance can easily be obtained. Such internal courses for engineers can reveal potential design talent within the ranks of the firm. Such people when they are spotted can be released for professional training. There is great value in the encouragement of internal recruitment of designers, but it is sometimes difficult for the firm to spot the talent without outside aid. The 'in house' man who has real design ability can make a major contribution provided management can give him the chance to spread his wings.

'In house' training presents a problem to the smaller firm with limited resources. One solution is for several small units to combine together in a group; if a bigger firm can also be persuaded to join, so much the better. This provides a useful pool of knowledge about design matters and a stimulus and exchange of ideas which are lacking in the smaller unit. It also introduces an element of competition which is healthy, without at the lower levels risking industrial security. This is an economic way of achieving results and can speed up the whole process of developing the young designer, who may also benefit from the challenge of external criticism of what to him are the established ways of doing things. It is naturally difficult to get such a course started but the principal of the nearest technical college can be the catalyst.

More is needed than just an expansion of knowledge; the essential factor is the improvement of creative design performance. It is this that so many mediocre design teams in engineering lack. In some cases a design appreciation course with an experienced tutor from outside may be needed just to establish that this lack is present. The manager can then go on to do something about it with the justifiable hope that his plans will be understood. A representative of Rolls-Royce at an engineering training conference suggested that what design education in engineering needed was the constant daily challenge to innovate which is so obviously present in an art school.

Art Schools
Few art schools nowadays are hidebound by convention and resistant to change, although some students find the syllabuses too departmentalised and rigid. The stimulus, however, to do something different, preferably your own thing, is dominant and it produces an unconventional, challenging type of young designer, slanted towards those industries producing goods which have a close relationship with people and must have a marked aesthetic appeal. They present the manager with almost the opposite problem from the aspiring engineering designer. The art school man or woman is eager to have a go at something new, impatient of attitudes and products which he believes to be out of date, often over-confident that he can assume design responsibility and perhaps lacking in knowledge of business practices—or so it seems to the manager. The art schools will rightly argue that they have only a limited time in which to develop the creative talents of the student, that stimulating creativity can only be done at the school stage and is unlikely to be engendered *ab initio* in the factory. Therefore the essential contribution of an art school is to produce creative people for industries which depend for their livelihood on a succession of new designs. This they try to do against a background of sound technique and logical processes. Maybe some art schools go too far in this innovatory role, training people to produce a greater degree of change than industry supposes its customers would swallow. Certainly there is a considerable wastage in the students the schools turn out. From the point of view of the manager this can be regarded as an *embarras de richesse*. He can pick and choose, but he must choose carefully.

For the design office he will want recruits who need holding back rather than pushing forward. Prodding designers into activity is never a very rewarding pastime. But it is undoubtedly a challenge to pick the candidate who has a genuine ability to produce new work and who is at the same time methodical and intelligent. Art schools now require a good standard of general education before training begins. The old gibe if Johnnie is no good at anything else but draws nicely, then send him to an art school to become a designer, is fortunately out of date. But it is true that some ex-students are still rather short on methodology and rely a trifle too much on subjective intuition (which Sir Hugh Casson, to redress the balance, calls instant rationalisation). The manager looking for an art school-trained designer will be looking for qualities which on the surface seem incompatible, a highly creative flair expressed through sound techniques and a nose for trends in design, yet an ability to work methodically in an organisation, respecting budgets and timetables. The art school claims to provide a lot of the flair and technique and a little of the method and accountability. The manager must trim his sails to that situation. His first concern is to spot the flair and technical competence and for this he relies on his own chief designer or, if he does not have one, an experienced outsider. Together they will examine the candidate's portfolio of work and judge its quality, asking questions which will expose knowledge and attitudes that are outside the scope of the copious formal cross-examination of the personnel manager whose main concern will be to eliminate the basically unqualified and the potentially unstable.

Choosing the Designer

The manager is alert to all clues that show past success, in however limited a context, which has some bearing on the career ahead. Designers tend to be individualists, and therein lies some of their strength, and they probably have more successful rogue elephants than most professions, but in the majority of people behavioural patterns are set up at a very early age and tend to repeat themselves. The manager will want evidence of highly imaginative work and also of an ability to approach a problem in the organised way described in chapter I. Badly presented work, however imaginative, will always be at a disadvantage because it hampers the designer's ability to communicate. An impressive portfolio, showing a reasonable spread of subject, can indicate two things, the

86

ability to present design information intelligibly and the ability to organise a job. If a portfolio seems to be all presentation of attractive results, the interviewer must press for a description of what the design brief was and how it was tackled, with what resources and within what sort of budget. Few young designers will come out of such cross-examination unscathed, but the course of the discussion will indicate what problem-solving capability the candidate has. The manager should not expect the complete answer that his own chief designer would give.

Bearing in mind that the design activity is teamwork, the temperament of the design candidate must be capable of accommodating itself to working with others in a constructive manner. A streak of individualism seems to be an essential part of most designers' psychological equipment. For a staff appointment an excess of it can be disastrous; a higher degree of temperament can be tolerated in a consultant whose contribution is often more of an individual character in problems of form and finish. At the other extreme the colourless, easygoing, anxious-to-please type is unlikely to cut much ice in a design team where a certain degree of tension is needed to sustain creativity. Usually it will be the larger firms which will have departments large enough to absorb annually a few recruits direct from college. Smaller firms will be seeking designers with some experience.

Normal recruiting and interviewing techniques by experienced personnel officers will apply to the appointment of more experienced designers. Portfolios will be more extensive and there will be completed products or graphics to be seen. One of the most difficult problems for the manager is to establish how much has been the direct responsibility of the candidate. It is not to be expected that all of it will be, because designing is so often teamwork, but the extent of involvement can usually be established by assessing the candidate's depth of knowledge of the whole design development. This can best be discovered by another experienced designer. Having stressed the need for a designer to communicate, it is perhaps also necessary to enter a *caveat* against the garrulous. Ability to communicate does not depend on the volume of words but on the content. A continuous flow of irrelevant conversation during design work can be destructive. Nor are words the only means of communication; the ability to sketch ideas freehand is a valuable part of a designer's professional stock in trade. A restless pencil can be better than a tireless tongue. The effectiveness of interviewing boards has recently come under fire, and it is as well to guard against the personal prejudices of individuals which are often exaggerated by the commanding heights of the interviewer compared with the applicant. There are professional interviewing techniques familiar to personnel officers which can be followed.

Choosing a designer can be a protracted time-consuming and expensive operation when costs of advertising and staff time are taken into account, as well as the inefficiency of a gap between a designer leaving and a new one effectively taking over the job. Here again the Design Council's well-tried service of selecting a short-list of designers for a nominal fee can save expense. Having examined the firm's problem the requirements are compared with the many hundreds of designers on the Design Council's records. A short-list of three or four names is then produced for the client, including some experienced and some younger designers. The client is advised to see all the short-list and not just plump for the first one if he seems all right. Designers need forewarning in order to assemble material for an interview and so a few days' notice should always be given. The manager may also find it more efficient and less embarrassing to have the portfolios delivered, if the designer is willing, the day before so that the contents can be carefully examined by the interviewers and their colleagues in advance, and a set of key questions prepared. Shuffling through a portfolio in front of a designer can be confusing to both parties.

Having prepared notes on each portfolio, it can be returned to the designer at the beginning of the interview so that an assessment can be made of his ability to present his own work. As the designer explains each job the manager can guide the interview according to the prepared notes. In most cases it is only fair to allow the designer to take away the portfolio at the end of the interview because he will need it at short notice for meetings with other potential clients. Staff who handle other designers' portfolios should have strict instructions to take meticulous care of the contents. Much of it is irreplaceable and the designer depends on it for his livelihood. In the case of consultant designers for an important assignment, a visit by one member of the interviewing board to the designer's office and studios can be a rewarding preliminary to appointment. Written references are not of great value in the appointment of designers. It is more satisfactory for staff appointments to ask for the name of two referees, one to be the present employer, and to promise to take them up only after first consulting the applicant when he is about to be offered the job and is known to be prepared to accept. Then a conversation on the phone with the referee is more revealing than a letter. The dodging of a question or the tone of voice can often provide a missing clue; the referee can then be tackled on a completely confidential basis without asking him to commit himself on paper. It is, however, wise to keep a note of the conversation on the file for future confidential reference.

When carrying out interviews to select designers it must be remembered that designers are professional practitioners governed if they are members by the professional code of practice of the Society of Industrial Artists and Designers, or their professional engineering institute. This code forbids the designer to work at the same time for clients in competition with one another without their agreement. Immediately it becomes apparent to the designer that he is being considered for work which competes with what he is doing for another client, he will discreetly but firmly want to clarify the situation. It is in the interests of the manager to be as helpful as possible in establishing the facts. Should it prove to be the case the designer will withdraw, if his existing client objects. The initial letters after his name on his letterheading should reveal the professional allegiance of the designer. In his own interest and as a matter of courtesy the manager should familiarise himself with these before meeting the designer. Some designers are on retainers from clients with an exclusivity clause which prevents them from working for clients in the same field. If, despite the competition, it is agreed by all concerned that the designer can work for both, this should be reflected in the contract to avoid misunderstanding at a later date. A designer is not debarred by his code from working on similar projects in the same field. This is a subtle distinction which depends on professional judgement.

A manager should also be aware that if he sacks one designer and tries to appoint another who is also a member of the Society of Industrial Artists and Designers, the second designer will consult with the first to obtain his agreement or at least to satisfy himself that the former appointment has been properly terminated. The manager will be acting correctly if he checks to which professional society each belongs and then comes clean if they happen to be the same. No useful purpose is served by secrecy. The second designer may otherwise find himself unwittingly in an unprofessional position, particularly if the manager is still arguing with the first about a final settlement of fees. The second designer will not be ganging up against you. He surely wants the job but he must behave correctly towards his professional colleagues. Equally the integrity of a designer is valuable to the manager who is therefore wise to be open about the situation. If such a situation is constantly recurring in his firm, he should have a close look internally; his own management of design may not be as professional as it should be. Any designer in the same society will take exactly the same line, and bad news soon gets around, such as withholding of payment from a professional designer for work completed in good faith.

On the other hand a designer's membership of the Society of Industrial Artists and Designers ensures that he will not divulge confidential information or publish the results of his work without his client's or his employer's consent. He will also declare a financial interest that he may have in any firm which may become involved in the design work, and he will not retain any discounts from contractors or suppliers, but pass them on to his clients. Nor will he knowingly plagiarise another manufacturer's designs. He will not advertise his services except for a salaried appointment, but he may send information to the press with his client's or employer's agreement. He can however allow his client to use his name in advertisements of factual statement concerning his work. This can be a considerable publicity advantage in some industries.

Competitions

One method of obtaining the services of a designer is by open competition. This is really no substitute for the routine methods already described. The open competition can be useful when a large concern is contemplating a new development and is short of ideas. A well-publicised competition can serve this purpose but it is not a cheap short cut to finding a designer in normal circumstances. A competition, however, might be justified if a firm wants to exploit a new material or a new technique. When planning a competition it is most important that the rules should conform with the principles agreed by the designers' professional societies. If the rules do not accord then designers who are members will not enter the competition. The manager can guard against this in the first place by seeking the advice of the Society of Industrial Artists and Designers or the professional engineering institutes which may also help to announce the competition if the rules are satisfactory. Competitions cannot be organised in a hurry as a last resort to get a firm out of an impasse. Not only have the rules to be agreed and printed, but they have to be widely circulated and then time allowed for busy people to prepare a submission. It is a mistake to imagine that most designers have the time and wish to enter competitions. They appeal mainly to young designers who want to establish their reputation. Established designers are usually busy and require a substantial inducement to give up their professional time for an unknown result. There is also a risk to their reputation if they are unsuccessful. For both the young and the established the basic requirement is that the financial reward offered should fully cover the cost of the time and material expended. The risk is taken because a well-organised and publicised competition brings the successful designer into the limelight and provides him with useful contacts. These attractions can be spread a little by the firm if there are some categories of commendation which give exposure to the runners-up.

The manager must have a reasonable budget for the printing and distribution of the rules, the reception and handling of the entries and their display to the judges, the exhibition and publicity for the results, and of course the prize money. Concerning the amount for the latter he will want some independent advice because the sum will vary according to the scope of the competition and the industry in which it is held. On this the manager may consult the Design Council which can be a powerful force in promoting sound competitions, and can also advise on the composition of the judging panel about which the Society of Industrial Artists and Designers will also have views. The competition may line up with the Design Council's own interests in encouraging designers, and it is worth trying to persuade the Council to sponsor it. In any case the competition should be advertised in *Design* magazine as well as other professional journals and also in the appropriate trade press. A press release should also be widely distributed for editorial publicity. Adequate text and pictures will be needed to publicise the results. Failure to do so can lose both the firm and the winner valuable publicity. The announcement of a competition needs to be supported by a full-scale public relations programme, otherwise the entries do not come in and relations with the design world are not improved.

The judges should be chosen with expert and external advice to establish the integrity and status of the competition. There must be a predominance of design experts among the judges and the firm itself should not seek more than one place which might well be filled from either design, marketing or production departments; if the winning design is to be of any use, it must be basically capable of production and also marketable. The budget will allow for a reasonable honorarium for the judges, their expenses and entertainment. If possible the date of the function when the results are to be announced should be agreed well in advance with the judges so that they are free to be interviewed by the press and take part in the event. The judges' comments can also provide copy for the press, and they should be provided throughout the judging with the necessary help to make a report. The judges will have their own views about the way they do the job, but a process of elimination provides the best basis, with a form of balloting in the unlikely event of disagreement concerning the final choice. Most judges will be sympathetic to advice from the sponsoring firm, but the manager will avoid trying to twist their distinguished arms. It is quite usual for a firm sponsoring a competition to retain the right to use any of the designs submitted, provided the proper rate for the job is paid to the designer. Equally there need be no obligation on the part of the firm to put into production the winning design. This is a delicate matter which needs careful handling.

A less usual way of obtaining a designer for an important task is the limited competition for which the organisation invites a few leading designers to submit designs. Each receives the same brief and each is paid the appropriate fee for the initial work which they do. It is not a cheap way of obtaining design work, but it does present the organisation with a choice of solutions in a situation where it is difficult to be very precise about the character required. The method is often used by prominent organisations who wish to demonstrate a degree of impartiality when making a new departure and also wish each solution under consideration to be backed by the name and experience of a well-known designer. Such is sometimes the case when a symbol of national importance or the elements of an international house style are required. When the Queen's Award for Industry was introduced the design of the symbol for the award itself was put out to limited competition. When such a galaxy of talent is assembled the organisation may rightly feel that it needs some outside expert to help in assessing the results.

The designers concerned will almost certainly be in touch with each other about the competition, so the manager need not adopt an attitude of secrecy concerning who has been invited. The designer's attitude will probably be that he will want to know who his competitors are when deciding whether to accept, but he will not of course relish everyone knowing of his entry if he does not win. This is one of the factors the designers will take into account when considering the invitation. If the task is not a highly desirable commission, the manager may find some reluctance to enter. A limited competition is not popular among designers, therefore the carrot must be big enough to overcome this. If it is a flop, the next step is rather awkward because the appropriate designer is surely not among those already invited and management must look elsewhere. However, a limited competition will not often be required, but if it is suggested, the design manager will be aware of the pros and cons of this rather delicate method of commissioning design work.

Contracts and Commissions

Having chosen the designer either by advertisement and interview, by personal recommendation or by competition, it is necessary to formalise the contract, the elements of which will have been discussed by both sides during the selection stage. In the case of staff designers, the firm will already have a salary structure into which payment of designers will have been fitted. Management's attitude to designer's salaries can be somewhat different from other posts. The firm will on most occasions require designers with outstanding potential; the geese that turn out to be swans will deal with routine work. The initial salary therefore should be attractive, but it is more important to have marked increases in the various grades so that a promising system of promotion is obvious. Useful designers are usually enterprising and ambitious. They embark on the career knowing that it is a high risk profession. Consequently they seek opportunities as much as high security. The salary structure should recognise this, knowing that the bright applicant will ultimately want to get on either elsewhere or on his own; the disappointments the firm will want to shed.

The manager who is aware of the central character of design work and the designer's need to integrate what he is doing with many other departments, will appreciate that status is important in initiating and sustaining relationships. So the new designer will be offered adequate status. It is better to provide this at the start, rather than begin to prop him up only when difficulties develop. A firm which is already project-oriented will have flexible methods of providing status rather than relying on the conventional pyramid and salary grades. The designer will also be more concerned than other staff about his working conditions because they will directly affect his work and he has been trained to be sensitive to them. A good general light and the provision of adaptable lighting (600 to 800 lux) for individual work places is now accepted as essential, along with work tables, drawing-boards and seating of adjustable dimensions and adequate storage for materials and drawings. It is worth paying attention to the general ambience of the office which should have a sufficient skeletal structure for the designer to be able to impose on it some reflection of his own personality. The aim of the management will be to provide sufficient open planning to facilitate communication and avoid isolation, while at the same time offering enough privacy to encourage the creative development of ideas. Distraction and peaks of sound are to be avoided. A sound level of about 50 decibels is quite tolerable (indeed some say essential) and the general level can be kept down by acoustic tiles, soft furnishing such as carpets and curtains which can also control sunlight. Access to daylight is essential for assessing colour ranges. Plants are to some degree sound-absorbent and have a beneficial psychological effect, provided they are kept healthy. There is advantage in giving designers the opportunity to participate in the treatment of their own working area, particularly in the selection of colours.

Dr Alex Moulton, in an address to a management conference organised by the *Financial Times* and the Design Council, describes his own arrangement of office space for his designers as a system of cells which allows immediate intercommunication, and at the same time permits intimate withdrawal to digest and define a new idea. This seems excellent for a small to medium design team, and in his case has produced some exceptional results.

The go-ahead young designer is interested in the firm's schemes for post-experience training and refresher courses. Disinterest can be taken as a bad sign. The more experienced designer wants to assess how he stands for promotion in relation to the chief designer and whether the firm has any history of promotion from the design office to other departments. Without making promises these aspects can be discussed quite openly. Another headache for management and staff designers is rigid office hours. They are really not very appropriate for designers engaged on creative work (or exhibitions) but naturally the firm must control working hours to some extent. One solution is to require so many hours a week to be worked and to have a method of accountability. A week is better than a day, because a designer developing a new idea may have to work intensively for two or three days and then need to relax. Reasonable allowance should also be made for designers to visit exhibitions both technical and art, particularly sculpture and graphics. A designer who gets permanently stuck in the corner of an office, never going places nor meeting people, will only exceptionally be doing himself or the firm any good. As in agriculture the best manure is the farmer's heel, so in a design office the amiable visit of the design manager is the best check on input. This can be compared with output which is the important factor, and the manager may be surprised to find that some of the more nonchalant input has a most rewarding output. Design work does not come by the yard, so management by results is perhaps the most useful guide. Remember the Bismarck quote in chapter 1.

Contracts with Consultant Designers

When dealing with freelance designers about costs, the first point to establish is their membership of a professional society, for example the Society of Industrial Artists and Designers or the relevant engineering institute. There may well be occasions when a designer outside a professional body can be commissioned, but when a manager does this he should always reassure himself about his professional reputation, but in most cases the designers in question will be members. Having established this, negotiations should respect that the designer is governed by a code of professional practice and discussions will continue on a basis of mutual trust. The next step is to create the right working atmosphere between the outside designer and the firm's own design or drawing-office staff. From the first moment that the suggestion is put forward for an outside designer to be brought in, the manager will encourage the assumption that the idea stems from the staff designers. This is not as difficult as it sounds, if the contribution of the outside designer is clearly identified with the interests of the resident staff. The consultant designer may be coming in to support and help implement what the staff designers have often recommended. He will heighten not decrease their status; he will not threaten anyone's job because he remains an outsider and he may well reveal to management an enlarged role for the resident design staff. This is the accurate and fair basis on which the manager can build.

When the attitudes are correctly adjusted then the manager can put his mind to establishing a formal relationship with the designer whom he is bringing in temporarily to supplement the skill of his own staff or to provide a service which for one good reason or another his firm does not have. Before arranging the preliminary discussion, the initial work on a design brief (see chapter I), will already have been done. Without an outline brief it is impossible to negotiate terms with your designer. The brief on the other hand may become modified as a result of the negotiations.

Preliminary Phase

Nearly every contract for design work can be conveniently divided into three phases:

A. The preliminary phase during which the designer pays several visits to the firm and discusses the brief with technical and marketing experts, surveys the problem in general terms and formulates ideas. Although this is a general examination of the problem the manager will structure it as precisely as possible, agreeing with the designer how many visits should be paid to the firm and arranging dates so that the appropriate people are available. He will prepare a list of key people to see internally and any outside suppliers or contractors. This will give some idea of how much of the designer's time, which is his yardstick of cost, will be needed at this stage. If a written report on what the designer discovers is required this should be formally agreed with the exact form in which the preliminary proposals will be presented (i.e. perspective drawings or models) and how many suggested solutions will be needed at this preliminary stage; one, two, three or more according to how precise is the brief. All this will affect the figure which the designer will put in for the first phase, and for which the manager will budget. It is the practice of designers to keep notes on all decisions of this kind and to keep records of the time spent on the activity. Likewise the manager will do the same.

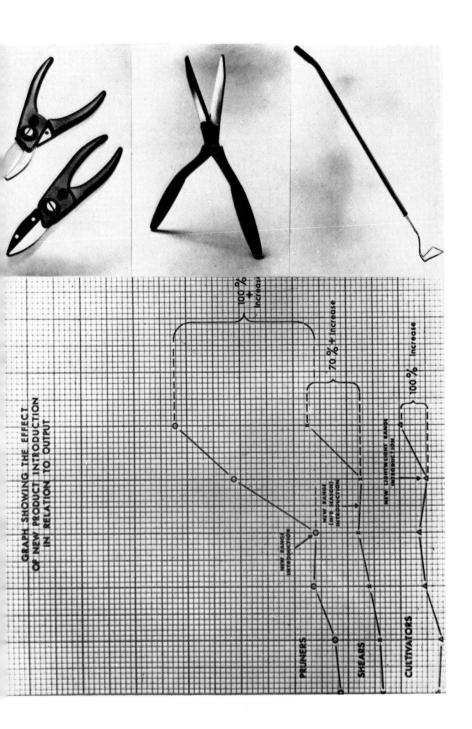

GRAPH SHOWING THE EFFECT
OF NEW PRODUCT INTRODUCTION
IN RELATION TO OUTPUT

100%
+
Increase

70%+ Increase

100% Increase

NEW RANGE
INTRODUCTION

NEW RANGE
(INTO SEASON)
INTRODUCTION

NEW LIGHTWEIGHT RANGE
INTRODUCTION

PRUNERS

SHEARS

CULTIVATORS

I

Normally the designer will write a letter setting out all he proposes to do at this phase and he will indicate what his fee will be up to the completion of the first phase, asking that it should be settled when that point is reached. In exhibition work, however, it is possible that the manager will give the designer a budget and ask him to work out what he can do within it.

The manager will reckon that for the time being he is investing in the designer and the designer in him. Moreover the manager will envisage the possibility that his briefing may prove to be inadequate. In that case the designer will have covered himself by quoting for time spent on alterations suggested by the client. The manager may even find that he cannot persuade higher management to adopt the designs suggested or possibly he himself could not recommend their adoption. Either way the manager will agree in the first stage with the designer a suitable breaking clause which will allow the termination of the contract on payment of the agreed fee at the end of the first phase. It is usually during this preliminary phase of exploration that fundamental difficulties become apparent either because the firm lacks the capability or the designer is unsuitable. Like the manager the designer does not want to be lumbered with an unproductive project, so the inclusion of a breaking clause is no embarrassment. It should, however, be envisaged that a change of direction may be indicated by this first phase and the contract will allow for the cost of recasting the preliminary sketches before the decision is taken to go ahead.

In this early phase the method of paying the designer will have to be agreed. This can be a lump sum payable say in three instalments with agreed allowance for extras, or it can be in the form of a sum plus royalties which will be a percentage of the selling price,[1] diminishing as the quantity sold increases. If the royalty system is adopted a method of audit and period of payment must be agreed and the designer will usually ask his accountant or solicitor to deal with this. In calculating royalties the manager can adopt the optimistic view that the design may be a bestseller, otherwise he may be in difficulties if it proves to be so, or it can be as a percentage of production costs, with the fee diminishing as the cost rises, an agreed proportion being paid at the end of each phase. This applies mostly to construction work like exhibitions and interior

[1] Dorothy Goslett, who has a great deal of experience in this field, suggests between 3 and 6 per cent in her book *The Professional Practice of Design.*

design and it is usual for a margin to be withheld from the contractor after completion to cover a liability for defects which will be assessed by the designer and the contractor after six months.

There is also the question of copyright to be settled at the beginning, because it arises as soon as the designer begins to produce solutions. The designer will want to retain the copyright of the work he produces at the end of phase A until you give him the go-ahead. If, however, much of the early work has been done in close co-operation with the firm's design staff, he is unlikely to make a point of retaining it. When the project enters the second phase the manager will want to have the full copyright of the designs which he has by then definitely commissioned. This will give him the right to change and to modify and he should certainly secure these rights for his company in the case of product design. In the graphic work the designer may impose some restriction such as an additional fee to be negotiated if the use of a symbol which he has devised is extended to other media. In any case the manager would be wise to consult the designer about this before altering the original design. In the case of a carpet the designer might require to be consulted about additional colourways. But these are qualifications which can usually be settled without difficulty. The main point is that the manager should not expect to control the copyright until he has paid for phase A and given the authority for the development of the chosen solution. He must also settle in the contract the form of credits to be given to the designer.

Development phase

B. The development phase will be dealt with in the contract, indicating what will be required in the way of development drawings, whether they will all be produced by the designer himself, or some or all by the firm's drawing office; whether models are needed and if so who makes and pays for these often expensive items. The manager may feel that he would prefer to have drawings first, and then if models are needed to negotiate them as an extra item. The scope of the development should be clearly defined to show, if a product, how many models are required to suit different markets or price ranges, if packaging, then how many sizes the design must be worked out in, or if a wallpaper how many colourways. The designer should not be expected to provide these variations from a fee which did not originally include them. The

98

manager will put into the contract the exact scope and form in which he wants results to be presented. If he is not sure he should be prepared to allow an extra fee for additional items. The manager commissioning a whole range of graphics which will amount to a house style or livery for the company, may wish to restrict the initial development to a few specified items such as a logotype, letter and bill headings, sales literature and van sides. These should be clearly listed to avoid misunderstanding. The designer will have to satisfy himself that his proposed logotype will be capable of reproduction in other ways later, such as newsprint and perhaps fabrics, so he will do some initial work on them but not develop them into a presentable form until he is required to do so.

Some target dates can also be negotiated for the development phase, but penalty clauses will not normally be necessary. The manager should be protected by a breaking clause which will allow him to settle fairly with the designer if the situation of the company should change in the meantime. It is much better to anticipate this unlikely event rather than try to find some ad hoc method of dealing with it should it arise. During development the designer will be keeping notes of alterations which are made at the firm's suggestion and agreeing them with the manager so that the fee can be adjusted. During the development there may be much exchange between the designer and the production engineers during which modifications may be suggested. The manager is quite justified in requiring that any major change is agreed through him as this may affect the contract and the budget. He can then decide whether the changes are at the designer's charge or the firm's. The regular progress meetings mentioned in chapter 1 should take care of these, until the presentation is made of the developed design solution which will be subjected to the process of evaluation. During this phase the manager will decide at what meetings it is essential to have the designer, and not waste the designer's time and his firm's money by having him at endless meetings from which he does not benefit.

Final Phase

C. The final phase will again specify the form, quantity and detail of working drawings to be submitted by the designer and specify what contribution will be made by the firm's own drawing-office. It will also define the designer's responsibility for checking the first batch of production

99

(or, if print, book proofs, etc.). The manager will then consider the problem of patents and of registering designs which is the specialised province of the patent agent.

The contract with the designer is the logical extension of the design brief. It may seem a ponderous affair but its preparation in meticulous detail can avoid a multitude of expensive and frustrating misunderstandings. The designer has to protect himself by inserting in the contract the definitions he requires; the manager will find it pays to do the same. This is not to say that tying a designer up in legal knots is a sound basis for creative work. But if the preparation of the contract is looked on by both sides as a marking out of the court on which both will play, rather than a series of trip wires, then it can be developed as a convenience which allows the job to go forward swiftly and smoothly. The contract will also provide a reassurance to the Jeremiahs who find it difficult to realise what the designers are doing as the time passes. It also is some reassurance to the manager who is new to design, that design work can in fact be managed.

Putting Work in Hand

Before finally buttoning up a formal agreement with a consultant designer, the problems of putting work in hand should be discussed. Where the firm is producing the design itself, it will usually have under its own control the facilities needed. The designer provides the drawings and specification and the relevant departments are instructed accordingly. There may, however, be exceptions if an unusual prototype is needed for which special materials and processes are required, and the firm does not intend to acquire them unless the prototype proves satisfactory. In such a case it may be wiser to have the job put out under the direct control of the designer. There are also other kinds of design work which a firm is not equipped to administer directly. It may be that the firm's requirement for print has been met by a jobbing printer with limited stocks of type and no typographical design service. At a moment of expansion the firm may require a series of technical leaflets for a new range of products for which a consultant designer has been commissioned. It is likely that neither the jobbing printer nor the firm's administrative or drawing-office staff are capable of seeing the job through satisfactorily. The printer may not have the type faces specified nor the skill to run complicated colour work if it is required. The office staff are unfamiliar with the techniques of ordering complicated print, checking and amending proofs and relating the invoices to the work done.

Similarly a firm may be undertaking a series of travelling exhibitions for the first time and has commissioned an outside designer to produce a plan for an exhibition unit which can be modified to suit several types of site. It is unlikely that the firm will have the resources to put out to tender, select the most suitable contract and supervise the work. The same might be true when a firm acquires new showroom space and employs a designer to plan the interior and the display. The work will probably be too specialised to be supervised by the staff administration which looks after the offices and the factory.

Rather than run the risk of an unsatisfactory result the manager will want his designer to act for him in seeing the job through to completion. He will have foreseen this final stage of the commission and borne it in mind when choosing his designer. He will also have satisfied himself that the designer has had the appropriate experience to do this. If the manager has any doubt about having the resources to supervise the job, he is well advised to ask the professional designer to do it for him. In exhibition, print and interior work particularly it is usually wise to go out to tender. To do this satisfactorily one must know which firms work to a similar standard so that their tenders can be compared (for example have a similar quality in finished work) and if they are not alike in what respect they are different so that due allowance can be made. The designer will know which contractors or printers in his line of specialism are well established and reliable although they may be high in price; which are cheaper but perhaps need more supervision or are cavalier about promised dates, and which are new, anxious for high-quality work and worth considering.

It may therefore pay the manager to retain the designer to select the firms who are asked to tender and to advise which to accept in order to get the most satisfactory result. The designer will not always suggest the lowest tender, which the manager might otherwise be tempted to do, because he sees some aspect of the tender which will lead to difficulty. If he turns a tender down on poor quality of work, the manager will rightly wonder why the firm was asked to tender in the first place; there may be a good reason. The designer then becomes the agent explaining to the contracting firm any special points of detail in the specification, possibly amending some aspect to meet the facilities of the firm doing

101

the job, instructing the successful one and notifying the remainder. The designer will be very conscious that he is your agent, looking after your interests, and he will require your agreement in writing to the final choice and to any important amendments which he finds necessary while the work is in progress.

The manager will want to know at what stages and on what dates his firm will be expected to settle bills, and he will want the designer to check and authorise payment first. The designer will pass on to his client any percentages he receives in commissions but he will add his own agreed fee for supervising the work. As a professional man the designer will also feel a responsibility to see that the contractors are fairly treated and promptly paid.

Most designers are passionately concerned to see that their designs are executed meticulously and on time. They gain considerable aesthetic satisfaction from seeing a job finally carried out to the standard they envisaged. The manager will find that his interest is best served by carrying the responsibility of the designer right through to the final completion whenever it can be justified. If the responsibility is switched at the ultimate stage to someone who does not fully grasp what is involved in the specification, it is tantamount to spoiling the ship for a hap'orth of tar. If for his own reasons the manager does not have the work finally supervised by the designer, he should always make sure that the designer sees the final result and receives the agreed credits, photographs of the work or samples if appropriate. To the designer each job is his passport to the next and he will wish to add this one to the portfolio which he produced for the first interview.

Many consultant designers work in partnerships of which the seniors are sometimes nationally or even internationally known for a personal skill of outstanding quality. If a manager is advised or decides to negotiate with such a partnership, it is a good move to arrange for the senior partner to discuss the project, if it is of sufficient size, with the senior designer at Board level. For the manager it is an opportunity to underline to the directors the importance and status of design work and to give the proposed project a degree of priority and support. It will also do the directors no harm to have to discuss the proposal with an acknowledged expert. They will have to do their homework and they may have their eyes opened to additional advantages which design work can bring. It would also help considerably if the chief staff designer is present. This will give him more power to his elbow when the project is put in hand and he is closely involved with other departments. Invariably the senior partner will wish him to be there. A great deal can be learnt about management by observing the way in which they treat their design staff, and the consultant designer will wish to take the measure of that problem if there is one. The chief designer's presence also makes it much easier for the consultant to integrate himself with the staff design office and reach an understanding from the first concerning the supporting, but not competitive, role of the consultant. Furthermore, the consultant will wish to be assured that if major difficulties arise he will have access to the Board. As mentioned earlier it is desirable if one member of the Board is particularly concerned with design matters; to him the design manager and the consultant can automatically turn.

Having involved the senior partner of a design consultancy in the policy discussions, the manager can discuss with him the extent of his personal involvement during the life of the project. Some managers are disappointed that the senior man seems to fade out of the picture all too soon. It is therefore best to agree at the beginning the points when the senior partner will be personally involved and tie him down to them. Such a man will be anxious for his younger designers to have a full range of opportunities and this is reasonable. On the other hand, the manager will rightly feel that he is paying for the man's skill and his name and wants reassurance that he is getting it. Having reached general agreement on this point, it is up to the manager to maintain regular contact with the senior partner and establish a friendly and constructive relationship. On a large project dates for occasional progress reports to the Board can be fixed well in advance and put in the diary of the senior partner who will want to keep himself up to date with progress. Such occasions can be profitably extended to build friendly bridges between top management and the design profession. The manager should not miss the opportunities which these meetings offer, not only to establish a rapport between the Board and the consultant but also to explore the scope of design innovation within the firm. Many a pigeon-holed idea has been resurrected at such meetings and has been argued through to a successful conclusion.

Design and Management Consultants
Another bridge which the design manager can usefully build is between

103

management consultants and design consultants. When firms of all sizes are faced with major reorganisation to meet change, they are finding that it pays to bring in management consultants to reconstruct some of the company's activities. The design manager is probably best placed to see the implication for design in a management consultant's recommendations. These may range from such broad matters as the individual responsibilities of directors to the strategy of product planning or packaging policy. The design aspect of such matters can easily be overlooked at the policy stage. As the management consultant works on these problems the manager can point out the relevance of the design function and at the appropriate moment arrange a meeting between the management and the design consultants. It is more convenient to do this when the management consultants are at work than to wait until the report is compiled and then argue the case through. The management consultant may be critical of a firm's economics of manufacture. Value engineering will go some way to suggest methods of improvement, but in many cases a complete reappraisal of a product range may be required as a preliminary to redesigning. There can be profitable co-operation between management and design consultants. Together they can more easily put into precise terms the cost/production ratio of a recommended development.

Michael Farr, the design management consultant, quotes a case where he was brought in by a firm of management consultants when a leading London laundry had to expand its market. A corporate image programme was decided upon and this factor alone contributed to a 40 per cent increase in their dry-cleaning business. In another case a management consultant may discern that there is a lack of continuity between research and development and the production line on the one hand and the requirements of the marketing division on the other. This could be due to a lack of appreciation of the design function in turning into hardware the needs of the market, using the company's resources for development. This would be a failure of design management which the management consultant could examine in more constructive detail with a design consultant.

It also works the other way. Many consultant designers who are brought in to reverse the falling curve of a sales graph, find that there is much more wrong with the firm's organisation than a lack of design talent. The company's objectives may be obscure; there may be confusion about what market the firm is really in; production may have become an end in itself with too little attention paid to the customer; or the whole process of decision making may have become obtuse. Before the designer can make much progress the management needs an overhaul and he may suggest that the co-operation of a management consultant is needed. The manager may himself be aware of this, but have already found that he cannot make any headway with the general problem. The introduction of an outside designer can stimulate the whole process of reassessment and the manager can then introduce into the situation a management consultant to carry the reorganisation into the heart of the company. Most management consultants are now convinced of the vital role of the design function, particularly in manufacturing industries. Bringing the two consultants together can make an effective impression on a Board of Directors, who have not allowed the design department to grow at the core of a firm during its expansion. This is often due to a failure to change attitudes at the top and it is from the top that initiative for the design function must come if it is to become a mainstream activity within the enterprise. When the manager is faced with a lack of support for the role of the designer, even though he has got as far as introducing a consultant designer, he may have to seek an opportunity to bring in the heavyweight management consultant who will recognise that the designers like other essential services can, given the chance, contribute greatly to the profitability of the firm.

Profit by Design

It is very easy for managers to find that their design department looks upon consultant designers as competitors, so the manager needs to be clear himself how to deal with the two complementary roles. The exact relationship will vary according to the size and progress of the company. For example, a technically minded young man (let us call him Mr Young) might start to make vacuum-formed garden pools in a disused greenhouse where temperature and humidity can easily be controlled. He begins this as a spare-time job, but due to his natural flair for promotion as well as methodical production this Mr Young finds a ready market for his product. After a couple of years he decides, with the financial help of his father, to give up his poorly paid salaried job and embark on full-time production with one assistant. He does a limited

105

amount of local advertising and arranges to supply several garden centres in the district. He soon finds that he is in a growing industry and is doing quite well. His pools manage to compete with those of larger concerns because his are designed principally for small children to paddle in. He had noticed that this is what his own two boys used his pool for. Mr Young therefore made his pools rather stronger and more stable, provided a broad rim for sitting on and made them easy to drain and clean. He produced an accompanying leaflet explaining these points to the customer.

After a further two years he found that the upward trend of the business was static, although he could still increase his production a little by employing another man. Other firms had begun to adopt his form of design and his approach to the customer. He felt that he could not safely cut his prices but that he must do something to enable his expansion to continue. Somehow his product must be more competitive. Mr Young noticed that his wife had just bought a set of plastic spoons in attractive subtle colours, with a black and white label attached with the legend, 'Selected for the Design Centre'. So he rang them up and eventually succeeded in explaining his problem to the right person, that he needed a designer. During the subsequent discussions he quickly came to see that he had not enough design work to employ a designer full-time, even one straight from the local art college. His needs would be better met by using a more experienced man as a consultant for the specific job of redesigning the pool. He was furnished with the names and addresses of three possible consultants and saw all three. The first he thought was too grand for his job and he hesitated to involve him; the third was bursting with too many ideas at once and he felt that he would be pulled in too many directions at the same time; the second had had some science specialisation at school but had gone to an art college and his quiet interested appraisal of the problem and some imaginative sketches which he made while he was talking convinced Mr Young that he was the man for him.

They agreed a limited project to amend the form to make the rim both stronger and more comfortable for sitting, and to revise the present range of colours which were battleship grey and an apple green which did not remain very constant throughout production. Mr Young was rather short of working capital at the time, so he suggested a modest basic fee to be paid in three stages and a royalty on the production. To his surprise the designer agreed, which implied that he had as much faith in the success of the business as Mr Young himself. The new rim was worked out without difficulty and a choice of four colours was taken from the British Standard Range. The designer argued that Mr Young might want to make other products for the garden and it would be convenient to extend the same colour range to them in order to avoid too much complication in running different colours and carrying stocks. Although different in colour (chroma) the four colours were in adjacent hues so that there was a compatibility between them. The customer therefore could have, if Mr Young eventually made them, several garden products made each of a different colour (chroma) but each having a colour harmony with the other. The designer explained that this would give Mr Young a good sales point, a flexibility in marketing and an incentive to the customer to buy more than one of his products. The designer asked that he should have for himself six samples of each colour from the first production run and Mr Young agreed.

In the exchange of letters it was also agreed that the designer should supervise the production of the first batch using Mr Young's labour. When they were successfully completed Mr Young was delighted and decided to have the designer replace his leaflet in colour. In a rush of enthusiasm he said he would leave it all to the designer who should use his own printer. The designer prepared the layout to a revised text ably written by Mrs Young, took estimates from two printers and wisely sent both to Mr Young with his own recommendation concerning which to accept. Mr Young was astonished at the cost of the colourwork, which he had no idea was so expensive, and became rather difficult. He was also concerned that the small swatches of colour attached were not the same as the colour of the pools which he could see in the yard outside his window. The designer explained that the colours were, within acceptable tolerances, exactly the same, that Mr Young was looking at the samples under a fluorescent light over his desk whereas the pools were in the daylight outside, and that the eye could not give an accurate colour impression from so small a swatch. The designer promised to produce colour swatches at least four inches square next time.

Mr Young was satisfied but still felt rather cheated by the colours until some weeks later his wife found with the aid of a chart in one of the Sunday colour supplements that her husband had slightly defective colour vision. Mr Young made a note that he would always work out proper budgets with the designer at the first stage, amending them later if necessary. The new range, after some initial scepticism at the garden shops about the lack of punch in the colours (they preferred the apple green saying that all gardens are green), went steadily ahead. At his wife's suggestion he sent a set up to the Design Centre which accepted them and showed them the following spring in the Centre for a modest charge, which was justified because a large hotel group saw them and placed a reasonable order for the gardens in their chain of hotels. The purchasing officer of the hotel group explained that they were the only ones in a decent range of colours.

Mr Young prospered for another four years. He expanded into larger premises, increased his plant and work force and set up a small sales department. He soon found that his salesmen needed more than children's pools to justify their existence and Mr Young remembered the designer's remarks about the colour range applying later to a wider range of products. He felt he needed some independent advice so he asked his original contact at the Design Centre if he could come down and see him. Together they agreed that the time had come for another stage of expansion based on a wider product range. Mr Young was confident that he had the resources, with the help of his bank manager, and he proposed to call in the consultant designer to start work. They discussed this at some length in relation to the future of the company for the next five years and together agreed that the consultant should be brought in to plan, for a fee, a new range of products, taking a long view of several years. At the same time Mr Young would engage a young staff designer with two or three years' experience since college. The youngster would have the advantage of working closely with the consultant from the beginning of the new product plan and would over eighteen months gradually take over the full design responsibility.

Mr Young worked out a draft plan for this, sent it to the consultant and asked him to come and discuss it with him. The consultant readily agreed to his role in the plan, but stressed that much depended on a satisfactory understanding being reached with the new staff man. They agreed that, as before, a short list should be provided by the Design Council, including one candidate who was, if possible, an ex-student of the local art college. It was also agreed that the consultant should be present at the interviews, for which he would be paid a fee. Everything

108

went according to the book and Mr Young found the ex-student he wanted. The consultant revealed that he had given lectures at the college in the department for three-dimensional design when the student had worked there. He spoke well of him and felt sure they would work satisfactorily together. During the first year the staff designer came on fast. New products for the garden such as terrace plant pots and some plastic coated chain link fencing went into production and were distributed through the same garden outlets. The sales force paid for its keep and the business expanded. At the end of the year when the consultant's contract came up for review, Mr Young was able to suggest that the consultant's visits should be cut down to once a month for six months and once a quarter for the following six months. If there were any unforeseen problems, the frequency could be modified. By the end of that year the consultant's involvement was reduced to an annual visit one month before the Annual General Meeting of what was now a medium-sized company. At the same time the staff designer was given an assistant draughtsman.

For the next ten years the firm continued to grow and prosper. Two smaller firms producing garden equipment were absorbed. The design department grew to cope with the expansion of their production into a co-ordinated product programme and the original staff designer became chief designer, after being detached for three months to work for a German firm which was not in competition. The chief designer was encouraged to do a weekly stint at the local art college when the previous consultant designer gave up lecturing due to pressure of work. The firm had gradually become much more engineering biased during its expansion and the chief production engineer undertook a similar task at the technical college. Three times a term they changed places and encouraged a little cross-fertilisation between the disciplines of technology and the arts. Mr Young became a governor of the College of Art, his company having won two awards for well-designed products, and being himself a speaker at several design conferences. There followed a further decade of prosperity and Mr Young became the chairman of what was now a sizable company. He had a little more time to think, he travelled frequently abroad and he was on the Confederation of British Industry Design Committee into which he put a new lease of life, with the assistance of his original consultant designer who there represented his professional society. Mr Young had the impression that his firm's products lacked edge. He saw with some dismay the proliferation of unrelated letterheadings, bills, invoices and other print. The annual report looked depressing in contrast to the healthy information inside. The whole image of the company lacked impact and vitality.

He went back to his friends at the Design Council and talked it over. It was time for the incursion of another consultant designer and he came away with his now familiar list of four names. He noticed that his original consultant was not on it. No doubt if that had been the solution he would himself have gone straight to him. But it was not. This new job of revitalising the design thinking of his company was the task for a younger man attuned to the requirements, technicalities and symbols of the future. He still respected his original consultant; they were now good friends. Mr Young saw all four names and he chose one from a consultancy of four designers all still in their thirties except their chairman who came from a leading firm of management consultants and was not a designer himself. The choice was fully justified, although Mr Young found that a lot more needed doing than he suspected. He ended up with a new chief designer because the job had really grown beyond the capabilities of his original man from the local art school. He had been moved sideways into the publicity department where he proved his worth dealing with all advertising and print. His place was taken by a graduate of the Royal College of Art with several years' experience in the electrical appliance industry. Some fat was lost in the design department and a print rationalisation programme was put in hand which reduced the total number of items by 12 per cent, cut the stationery bill and simplified the stock taking.

Before long the consultant designer had told Mr Young that he thought there was a good case for management consultants to take a look at the interaction between production and marketing. He believed that this was responsible for much unnecessary redesigning in the design department. This was done and the design department was placed under the director of marketing who himself had a degree in mechanical sciences.

Mr Young realised that he had started something larger than he expected. He had from the start tried, with appropriate professional advice, to keep the design function in step with other sides of his business, sometimes perhaps a little ahead. He missed the old days in the greenhouse with his small enthusiastic team. Now it seemed he had almost designed himself out of a job. He started to take part-time directorships in other companies and began poking his nose into their design departments. His old spirit revived and he started to look years younger.

The Nature of Creativity

Throughout this account of the design process great emphasis has been put on choosing designers with creative ability and on management stimulating the creativity of the design department. This means abandoning some of the conventional attitudes towards staff behaviour. Mr Saul Bass the distinguished American designer who is also a Royal Designer for Industry has pointed out: 'The creative personality is essentially nonconforming. If we understand the creative act to be an insight that establishes a new relation between existing concepts or objects, then we must accept the fact that to one degree or another each creative act is a nonconformist act.' He also explains why management must budget for a margin of designs which are abandoned at the evaluation stage and why the designer needs status and management support. 'One of the problems of the creative personality is the spectre that "newness" may mean failure. In such a success-oriented world, the concept of failure looms as a fate worse than death. Yet failure is built into creativity. If the creative act involves this element of "newness" and "experimentalism" then one must accept the possibility of failure. So not only must we have the opportunity to nonconform, but we must have the opportunity to fail.' George Bernard Shaw as usual went one further: 'Reasonable people adapt themselves to the world. Unreasonable people adapt the world to them. All progress is made by unreasonable people.' By now the design manager will not expect design management to be all sweet reasonableness, but his task will be easier if he is trying to manage. Mr Saul Bass does not pretend to understand fully the complex process of creativity, but his experience suggests four preconditions that must obtain for the process to occur.

First, there must be an ability to project a non-existent imaginary world—a fantasy world. Second, there must be the ability to live consistently and logically in this world; to explore it fully and freely, albeit based on an arbitrary (perhaps even illogical) premise. Third, there must be the ability to enter and leave this world at will (if you can't do

111

this you are not creating—you are emotionally disturbed) and finally there must be the ability to edit the experiences gained in this world and to assess their relevance to the problem at hand.

Mr Bass has support for the intuitive contribution of the designer from Sir Barnes Wallis: 'It is not difficult to find examples that show the overwhelming importance of intuitive judgement to any technologist engaged in any potentially dangerous undertaking that involves creative work; indeed it may be the factor that determines the issue of success or failure, of life or death; and not for himself alone but of others who may be joined with him.' He blames the education system for discouraging intuitive judgement by putting too much emphasis on 'close-ended questions' which are those that have only one correct answer. Many technological problems, however, are 'open-ended' questions to which there are more than one, and may indeed be many, equally correct answers. I mentioned earlier the value to creative work of the free atmosphere of the art school. Sir Barnes Wallis points out that Dr Hudson when examining results from American tests of creativity found a surprisingly sharp arts/science discrimination. Arts specialists seem to find that suggesting uses for objects was congenial and relatively easy to do. But nearly all the young physical science specialists, gifted and weak alike, found these tasks antipathetic. The tenor of scientific education as a whole is antipathetic to problems which do not have single right answers. From an early age scientists are not trained to think in a wide-ranging manner around practical or intellectual problems, but to search methodically for the correct, the best solution—in other words to 'converge'. In contrast the arts specialists seem prone to think 'divergently' and are probably encouraged by their teachers to so do. In America divergent thinking is associated with originality and 'convergent' thinking with dull uniformity. Frequently, technological problems are unlike those of pure science; frequently they are susceptible to more than one good solution. And for this reason they may demand flexibility and imaginativeness over a wider range than required of the scientist in pure research. Conventional sixth-form science teaching may well encourage in boys destined for careers in technology a rigidity of mind which unfits them for this work.

Sir Barnes Wallis reminds us that certain criteria of creativity were suggested by Dr Arthur Koestler at the 1965 meeting of the British

112

Association. These are '(*a*) originality, (*b*) the previous unrelatedness of the matrices which enter into combination; which, he says, may somewhat loosely be called "the improbability of the combination" and (*c*) the intervention of the extra-conscious process'. This is supported by Mr G. Sommerhoff of University College London who suggests that the intuitive faculty only comes into effective operation if and when we have, either of set purpose or it may be by chance, suppressed for a time our conscious reasoning process; for our conscious reasoning may be, and indeed frequently is, at fault.

Encouraging creativity among creative designers may, therefore, lead the manager into some strange situations which will test his own open-mindedness and perspicacity. On occasions he may have to persevere patiently in order to understand what the designers are getting at and then help them put it across to their colleagues. If he is in search of progress he may find comfort in the observation of G.B.S.

Chapter 4

Design and Corporate Identity

Having mastered the design process and related it to the company's objectives, having selected designers and discovered how to get the best out of them, the manager can put his mind to the co-ordination of all aspects of design activities within his organisation. When he has organised professionally the various sections of design work such as product, presentation, print and premises, there is the further possibility of interrelating them so that they create a strong and effective corporate identity which can assist the firm in its marketing and reinforce the loyalty of the staff. This is an area of design management which is becoming increasingly interesting to firms as they grow larger and compete for ever greater numbers of customers, and consequently become concerned about their impact on the community at large. Competition tends to equalise the basic technical and commercial advantages and emphasises marginal characteristics. The personality of an organisation or its corporate identity then becomes important in its promotional activity. This personality can influence public attitudes not only at the point of sale but also when the company is competing in the market for good quality personnel or negotiating with social and other institutions for permission to construct, to receive financial support or obtain credit.

There usually comes a moment when a senior manager looks around him and instead of seeing, in visual terms, a well co-ordinated obviously efficient undertaking, he is confronted by a sprawling amorphous collection of odds and ends which have accumulated over years of successful expansion. Buildings have been added and extended without any overall architectural plan, premises have been acquired with widely different characteristics, showrooms and reception areas bear little resemblance to each other, lettering on fascias, van sides, notice boards and signposts have no common typography, letterheads for stationery, invoices, bills and labels are as diverse as a book of type faces. The total effect suggests disorganisation and inefficiency. The outward impression probably reflects a degree of underlying truth.

The initial reaction of management to this discovery may be that everything needs a face lift. Some improvement can indeed be achieved by standardising public lettering, a type face for print and colours used for paintwork and soft furnishings. But this is to tackle the symptom rather than the cause and fall short of a total corporate identity programme which will promote the company both outwardly to the public and inwardly to the staff in a manner most appropriate to the company's needs. Moreover such changes cost a considerable amount of money, even in a medium-sized organisation, so it is better to survey the whole problem thoroughly in order to produce a properly co-ordinated programme which can serve for a decade and more with only minor alterations.

Once the manager has turned his mind to the problem, he will probably be appalled by the extent of what has to be done. The items which need attention will produce a list as long as his arm; to do them all, he assumes, would cost a mint of money, and he will wonder by what guiding rule he should proceed. To some extent he can define the problem in managerial terms because it is a case of confusion and disorganisation. He will find that much of the visual confusion arises from a lack of rationalisation, because the disorderliness he can see around him expresses a lack of thought by staff who have taken ad hoc decisions without reference to the total effect. So the manager can take rationalisation as his watchword. He can start to carry out a programme of rationalisation for all the visual manifestations of his organisation. The Board will find this a reasonable task to undertake and it should not be difficult to gain support in principle for an ultimate result which will give the company an appropriate and attractive corporate identity. Most directors are sensitive to the effect the company's activities have on the public mind and believe that a clear identity and a benign personality, expressing both efficiency and reliability, are an asset to the general conduct of business. The company will probably have a public relations activity already which is working to attract attention to the company and present it in the most favourable light. As Sir Paul Reilly has said, an imaginative and well-designed corporate identity programme is something which P.R.O.s dream about but do not often get.

Design Survey

The Board, however, will want to know what resources will be required to achieve the corporate identity and at what rate they will have to be made available, and as the programme is based on rationalisation what advantages and savings will accrue. Having won outline approval for the idea the manager will have to produce his plan. This is difficult not only because the scope of the project is so wide, but also because internal staff cannot easily be objective about the subject. The outsider is much more capable of seeing the incongruities and the illogicalities, and of having the authority to substitute more rational procedures. For a corporate identity programme the manager will need an outside consultant designer more than for any other form of design work. He will now be familiar with the method of selecting the most suitable designer, but he will be wise in this case to commission from the designer a preliminary survey with recommendations of what must be done and in what order. He may be unwilling to commit himself to a full reorganisation from the start, if to do so would risk dislocating the organisation, or failing to obtain the degree of staff co-operation necessary or spending too much money in one financial year. Instead he can choose a designer who has some experience of the work and has proved that he has enough creative imagination to produce a distinctive house style unlike competitors. He will ask him to examine quickly but thoroughly all the visible manifestations which affect the company's public and its staff, with a view to facilitating its manifold operations and improving goodwill both externally and internally.

Before the consultant designer can begin on his first phase of a survey, for which an appropriate fee is agreed, the manager will collect a body of relevant information. First of all the designer wants a comprehensive list of all forms of correspondence and notification, advertising, publicity, promotional literature, labels and other methods of identification, packaging, display and exhibition material, signwriting for fascias, notices, signposts, van sides, house colours, symbols, trade marks, badges, uniforms, architecture and decorative schemes, ranges of products and services. He will also want a list of heads of departments which have any responsibility for the production or use of visual communications. This will also include dealers and agents and other local, national and international contacts whose opinions may be useful: what is eye catching in Brighton may be downright offensive in Bangkok. He will also need a comprehensive collection of actual examples of all the company's current print, from letterheading to publicity material. This collection may be an eye-opener to the manager and will usually demonstrate more forcibly than anything else the need for a programme of rationalisation. These three categories of information will provide the nucleus for the designer's survey and enable him to start.

The manager will stress the importance of the relationship between the company's activities and the visual items used in these activities. Management devises control systems for organising its resources which are economic, technological and aesthetic, in order to create, through the design process, results which are profitable to the enterprise.

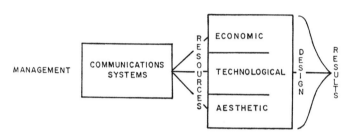

Figure 12

Most of the items used to achieve results will be an amalgam of those three resources in differing proportions. For example machine tools used in the factory will have a high technological and economic content but still some aesthetic content to make them easy and safe to operate and maintain by the workers. The forms in the accounts department are technically highly organised, the economic outlay is comparatively small, but the aesthetic aspect will be important in order to make them convenient and quick to use avoiding error and fatigue by layout and legibility. By appreciating the aesthetic (or human factor) element in each item a pervasive design characteristic can be developed which in sum will amount to a corporate identity. Contrariwise a neglect of this common element can lead to overall visual confusion. The designer identifies these elements and organises them rationally and efficiently. He will find that in a high proportion of items there is a graphic/communications element and a colour element which may be used to communicate information, as in safety systems, to identify categories or to contribute to the environment. Consequently, the two main factors in organising a corporate identity system will be form and colours which can bring into congruity items as divergent as transport and billheads.

Successful Examples

The way for the designer will need some preparation and the first essential is full co-operation from the Board and its overt authority for the designer to investigate all aspects of the problem at whatever level. The manager may have to put some initial hard work into this and produce some evidence from industrialists who have successfully instituted design policies of this kind. Sir Arthur Norman of De la Rue has confirmed: 'Once the standard has been raised, the company image acts as a deterrent to slovenly work, shoddy design and poor services, and as a magnet as well to young people who want to enter industry by joining a firm with obviously high standards and a modern outlook.' Over fifteen years ago Olivetti were able to claim:

It is a special feature of our company that the work of designers cannot be considered in isolation from the general life and thought of the organisation which gives all its activities a special quality. It is probably too early to claim that Olivetti has achieved the complete assimilation of the aesthetic, but that we are progressively moving towards it is certainly true. Already the company has a personality which is identifiable not only in its products, but in its advertising, buildings and equipment. That is not to say a lot of clever artistic men have built up an image which the public called Olivetti's, but rather that a mature organisation had been created—certainly with the help of aesthetics— which our designers and artists have interpreted in an unmistakable, perhaps even inevitable way. Design does not now stop when designers go home, but has become an instinctive part of the company, playing its part as much in the manufacture of a link for a calculating machine as in the organisation of an accounts department.

The same conception has been put by one of Britain's most experienced consultant designers, Professor Misha Black:

Design in an industrial organisation is not a question of one brilliant idea or even a series of creative bombshells. It is the slow permeation of a visual sensitivity through every aspect of the firm's work, from the

118

product itself to the point of sales dispenser, from the architecture of the factory to the uniform of the truck driver, from the furnishing of the chairman's office to the fittings in the operators' washroom.

This pervasive attitude towards design permeating through the fibres of an organisation rather than being, as Hans Gugelot put it, icing poured over half-baked cakes, is becoming the normal attitude of top management to design work. If the manager finds that this is not even beginning to be accepted by his own Board he will have an uphill but not impossible task. Much can be done on the basis that logical re-organisation is needed and change is overdue, change as always being the opportunity for improvement, even improvement by stealth. But the situation can be improved if the consultant designer is given the opportunity to argue his own case with the Board. Often he will find an alignment of interest with the director responsible for long-range planning. Arthur Earle, as head of the London Business School, put the job firmly on the shoulders of designers not to let management duck changes. He went so far as to say:

For my part I would urge upon management the thought that the presence of the designer in the planning team is of critical importance to its success. His is precisely the sort of free-ranging mind that is creative in brainstorming sessions and his the most discerning pair of eyes to perceive the ways in which a given company's skill and resources may be applied in new ways.

Preparing for a corporate identity programme can be the beginning of a fundamental phase of change in a company's development. It, therefore, needs careful timing by the manager. As Mr Fei of Olivetti suggested it is a sign of a company's maturity. I suspect it only occurs in the stages of early development when the organisation is led by a professional designer such as Terence Conran, who has established thorough design policies in his companies from their inception.

Benefits
While appreciating what the designer is trying to achieve and how he will do it, the manager can leave the technicalities to the designer, but he himself will be constantly seeking the fruits of rationalisation in the form of simpler administrative procedures, variety reduction of items

119

used, economies in cost and time and improved effectiveness in business transacted. A pretty face undoubtedly raises morale; it should also be able, in the long run, to attract the customer. Different departments in the company will obtain different benefits from the corporate identity programme; to some it will be the cost advantage, to others it will be greater simplification, to yet others it will be more effective impact on the customer or an improved climate in which to do business. The manager ensures that each section is aware what benefits will come to them, and enlists their co-operation. The manager following in the wake of the designer's survey will find endless opportunities for improvements which have been revealed in the survey and of which he can take advantage. The designer may chart the activity of departments and the way they interrelate with other departments in a form which surprises the manager, but is in fact nearer to the truth of what actually happens.

Henrion Design Associates were commissioned to examine the problem of design co-ordination in the Post Office as part of a reorganisation plan, in order to establish a manageable structure. After extensive investigation at all levels they produced a list of design items which had been mentioned by each department, noting the connection between them, and arranging them in design groups. Mr Henrion observed that these groups cut across the administrative grouping:

> For example, pillar boxes, telephone kiosks and stamp vending machines might be sited on the street side by side, and should hence be closely co-ordinated (even to the extent of considering a combined unit); but administratively these are controlled by three separate branches with no formal co-ordination. On the other hand, we felt that the design of 'public information' should be more sharply distinguished from 'promotion' than the administrative structure would suggest. The diagram opposite shows the designer's grouping (figure 13).

During the survey the designer will demonstrate what sort of identity the firm's existing visual manifestations present both to the public and the staff. The main impression will probably be contradiction and confusion. Then the manager must be prepared to state what characteristics the Board wishes to emphasise. Most companies will wish to portray the usual virtues of integrity, reliability and efficiency, but will at the same time want to appear distinctive. Some effort will be made to define to the designer what that difference is. This individuality is given form by the

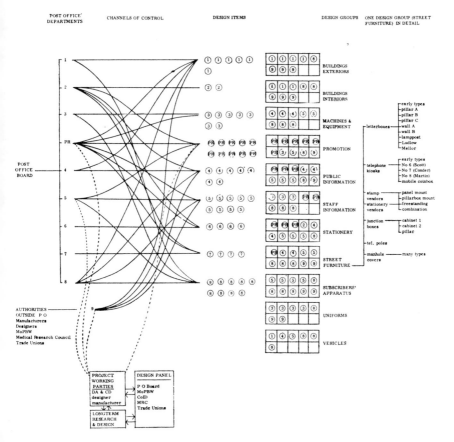

Figure 13

designer's creative imagination. When a design is first presented to management, it may seem strange, provoking the slightly illogical comment that it is too unconventional. Presumably a conventional proposal would attract the comment that the style was too similar to the liveries of other companies. It is as well, therefore, for the design manager to work closely with the designer at the stage of creating symbols, logotypes, house colours and letterheadings, acting as a sieve between the designer and the Board who will be very sensitive to the visual trappings which the company is being invited to wear, no matter how indifferent they have been to the tatterdemalion assortment in which they have acquiesced for so long previously. Many distinguished symbols for

121

companies have seemed strange at first sight, but their appeal increases with acquaintance as the full range of their application becomes apparent. The manager is wise, therefore, to be meticulous about the presentation of a scheme to his colleagues, making sure that it is as complete and professional as possible. Nor will he press for quick decisions, but give time for the initial shock to mellow into a kind of affection. This is what happens with the general public and why, having established a livery, it is so difficult for a company to decide upon changes.

When F. H. K. Henrion first designed the new emblem for BEA to express, according to his brief, nationality and flight, many were critical of the strong visual impact of the Union Jack converted into an arrow, with a streamlined logotype to go with it. However BEA, with its long experience of the subject, did not lose its nerve and soon the recognition value and distinction of the design was accepted. BEA's experience also enabled them to apply it to aircraft, vehicles, buildings and print without delay, and yet within the normal programme of repainting and restocking, an exemplary combination of design and management skills. (Details on pages 132–3.)

The survey shows what is being done at present and how it is being done, but it also indicates what is not being done. There may be items which a section of the public are aware of, that carry no memorable mark of the company's identity, a target area which is being missed altogether. There may be separate identities within the group which could benefit from a visual link with the parent body. Sometimes the reverse may be the case, particularly when manufacturing units are established in foreign countries where national rather than international identity is required. Some of the existing elements may logically form the basis of a new corporate scheme or a completely new start may be needed. The contribution which buildings and architecture can make may have been wholly neglected. It will probably also be clear that there is no central control to establish scope, consistency or budgeting. The survey, however, will reveal the dimensions of the problem, the extent of reorganisation required to institute an efficient scheme and a rough indication of total cost.

The extent of the corporate identity programme should relate precisely to the needs of the company. Some firms want it to extend widely to all sectors of the public, to include all potential customers and suppliers, local and central government, banks and agencies as well as employees at all levels. Others want to restrict the recognition of the parent company to a limited sphere of governmental and financial organisations and shareholders, leaving subsidiaries to establish their own identity and brand images. Or it may be a mixture of both, comprising identification with the parent but in a manner subordinate to the separate companies' identities. These relationships need careful definition before design work begins. The problem of control also has to be faced in the early stages because it is all too easy to work out an elaborate system for corporate identity and then have no means of implementing it and controlling it year by year. Considerable authority is needed to put the programme into operation, then to preserve its essentials during the course of its life. No scheme can remain indefinitely in a strait jacket; it must be capable of amendment, addition and modification as circumstances change. Powerful supervision is needed if the corporate identity is not to become frayed at the edges and eventually disintegrate. It is like an interior furnishing design; unless the housekeeping is strict, unsuitable additions are brought in, repairs are done which do not match the original work and modifications are made by amateurs, until the whole area loses its original distinction. If management is not prepared to exercise the necessary control for a thorough scheme, it is better to limit the plan to the bare essentials and monitor those satisfactorily.

Print

Few firms would not benefit from a programme to redesign their print, and this is often the logical starting-point and easiest approach to a corporate identity. Print is constantly being reordered anyway; there is an established budget for it; redesign can be introduced without much dislocation and the results are far reaching. If print is chosen some budgetary allowance can be made for the designer to explore the application of logotypes and symbols to other materials than paper and in larger and even smaller sizes, so that the scheme can be extended when required. The most difficult, as well as the key, item is the letterheading. Top management may have highly individual views about what is appropriate to their status. The chairman may indeed want a special version. At the other end of the line the typist must not be set inconvenient, and thus wasteful, problems of alignment and registration.

Standing orders for a typing style and the design of a letterheading should be worked out together. Some departments will want particular sizes of paper and methods of production varying from electric typewriting to duplicating. There may be special headings for some classes of distribution. All this is capable of rationalisation into a standard heading with a limited number of variations. Each demand for a variation will be deeply scrutinised by the manager and designer before it is accepted. The motives for having something special are strong and not not always justified. The manager for his part will insist that items of information on the heading are clearly displayed and that sources of confusion are avoided, particularly in the case of postal codes and telephone numbers. The latter should be easily identified as they can be constant sources of error.

Service Industries and Print

The letterheading will not be designed in isolation but as the cornerstone of a graphic style for the company, which in turn is part of the whole communication system of the organisation to its customers on the one hand and to its staff, agents and suppliers on the other. All communications are not graphic but visible communications are among the most constant and enduring. They can be particularly effective in reshaping the lines of communication following mergers, take-overs and regroupings.

It was the merger of the Clydesdale Bank and the North of Scotland Bank that prompted their decision to modernise themselves and undertake a complete programme of rationalisation for their print. The change in name automatically meant that stationery, documents and leaflets would have to be reprinted. For some time they had realised that they could no longer afford to wait until customers came to them; they would have to go out and persuade them. A corporate identity was obviously needed for the new organisation and consultant designers were called in to plan a programme with three elements, a house style for all correspondence, a symbol as a linking device in all print and the use of international standard paper sizes. The designers began with the cheques, 24 million of which were issued every year; it bore the symbol and its colour was adopted as the house colour. The management anticipated that its customers, mostly limited companies, would resist, but in the event there was very little opposition. The heading of the letter was then redesigned, and the layout was standard for all letters and circulars. When the programme was complete over 1,100 forms had been redesigned and about 160 had been eliminated. Printing was centralised in new premises with modern machines and new layouts. Over half the stationery was then printed on international paper sizes using three sizes instead of nine previously; the remainder could not initially be printed in these sizes due to computer accounting and inter-bank requirements. The new layout achieved easier use, easier filing and economy in stocking. For all print layout a grid based on a nine-point modular system was used.

The symbol (plate II, facing p. 97) could be used in a variety of sizes, on letterheads in print or blind embossed, silk screened on a diversity of materials and it was also successfully applied to the buildings in the main strees, to advertising material, booklets, book matches, ashtrays, playing cards, statement holders, cheque wallets and coin bags. The house colour was successfully used for the girls' dresses. Although the initial programme was concerned with the rationalisation and design of forms and documents, as it progressed the brief was extended to cover other ways in which the bank's personality is impressed on the minds of the public. (Cf. the neat way the FMC logotype, facing p. 97, suggests *their* personality.)

Mr R. D. Fairbairn, Director and General Manager of the bank, comparing the five years before the new corporate identity was introduced with the five years following, was able to claim that:

> . . . growth as measured by deposits relative to other Scottish banks showed a margin of 3 per cent in the second period. Looking at the number of customers we find that during the first period of five years the number of accounts rose by 16 per cent and during the second period the number increased by 25 per cent. I think it would be fair to give design some credit for this good performance.

The foregoing shows that the skilful management of the design process, carried out by professional designers, can make a substantial contribution to the effectiveness of service industries which have no manufactured product to sell. Indeed it can be argued that it is businesses which offer services that have the greatest need for an imaginatively designed corporate identity. The benefit comes not only from the

125

corporate identity itself but also from the improvements which stem from a close investigation of the whole business operation. The same applies to air and shipping lines, catering groups, insurance companies and retail businesses.

Over recent years we have been able to see how the concern of the Design Director of British Railways has improved the comfort of the paying passenger; an example of a very small department influencing the buying habits of a huge organisation backed by the strong support of convinced top management. Lord Beeching, as chairman of the British Railways Board, regarded a design policy as a means of achieving customer satisfaction:

No modern commercial undertaking, particularly a large one can fail to benefit from a constructive attitude towards industrial design. In the world of public transport we are continually striving to present ourselves to best advantage by combining functional suitability with modern aesthetic standards. Good design results in economy in capital expenditure, earns public respect, helps to induce custom and contributes to the presentation of a favourable image. Design is a management responsibility. In a large and complex organisation, the management of design must inevitably be indirect, but it must be continuous and cover all aspects of the concern. . . . The railways have never before had to consider so closely, or deeply, the objectives which are essential to their survival. Design is important in so far as it contributes to those aims. . . . We are well aware that our success in the future will depend to a great extent on what the public thinks of us and the public's thoughts will be largely formed by the things they see and use. From the appearance of a locomotive to the cut of a porter's coat, from a freight symbol to the planning and design of a ship—everything that we use that is right for its purpose and is truly modern in design is a help. Everything without these qualities is a hindrance.

Control

This puts succinctly the objective and scope of design and a corporate image for a large service organisation which at that time was urgently in need of revitalisation. It shows the pervasive rather than superficial attitude of management towards the design function, indicating that design policy is closely related to company strategy and company philosophy. When such a policy is adopted with conviction in all its wide implications, management has the problem not only of planning and creating the corporate identity programme, but also of controlling it. This complex problem of control has to be thought through as the scope and content of the programme is devised so that a practical set of procedures is compiled to maintain the essential elements of the system. Clearly the first element of control is authority from the top. If the corporate identity is interpreted by middle management as an inconvenient frill which does not much matter, the result will soon lack all cohesion and impact. Senior managers can make evident their concern and treat it as a serious aspect of the company's operations. It should not be difficult to enlist the support of the publicity manager, who will appreciate the value of visual communication. There may, however, be some difficulty on the administrative and technical sides, whose co-operation is also important. To them the contribution to rationalisation and organisational convenience will have most appeal, and the proposals can be put to them in that light, although ultimately the aim will be to achieve the total climate of understanding and teamwork which Mr Grindley describes on page 136.

The manager now has the job of developing alongside the design programme a system of control. It is often sound to centralise the control where most benefit is gained from the programme. For this reason some organisations make the director of marketing responsible for it, as in BEA. This obviously creates an external, public relations, marketing bias and steps have to be taken to ensure that other, more internal, aspects are not neglected. Alternatively, the design manager himself may control the programme and from his impartial position make sure that the various aspects are co-ordinated to achieve the total effect. Either way it will be necessary to assemble together the bones of the system—the master drawings, the colour swatches, the typographical instructions, the signwriting and painting specifications, and the schedules of fittings, furniture and furnishings. These can be organised into a design manual by the designers, and made available to all those who have any responsibility for implementing the corporate identity programme. It can be introduced at a briefing session when the designers are present and top management is seen to be supporting it.

The manual can be built up in sections as the programme is extended

127

until the optimum effort is being put into it to produce effective results. The manager will sort out with the designers and the staff involved which elements must be regarded as mandatory and used in the prescribed forms at all times and which are allowed some flexibility to meet local conditions or new situations. The programme may give strong visual character to a parent company but at the same time admit subsidiary elements which allow regional or functional groupings to be identified. Such variations can be a headache to management, but are often justified. Provided they are designed into the system and proposals to use variations are notified to the design manager, there should not be much difficulty in keeping the bold outlines of the scheme without fraying the edges, and at the same time benefiting from regional pride which may be a consideration in the company's overall policy.

We can now assume that the manager has accepted the survey and decided which is his priority area, such as print, and adopted the organisational procedures set out in chapter 1 for managing the design process; that is a policy group initiating a design brief, a design team, and an evaluation group linked to the policy group. Throughout the process he will have found that evaluation is less easy to assess in a corporate identity programme than in developing a product; feedback from the customer is not readily quantified. He will, however, have gained internal advantages in administrative procedures and variety reduction and other aspects of rationalisation. But he cannot evaluate total success upon the internal advantages. It is quite possible to achieve a high degree of rationalisation, but still miss the impact, recognition value and memorability which stems from the designer's imaginative skill in manipulating the two main elements of any corporate identity; the cumulative results of the repetition of the selected motifs; and the effective combination of symbol, typography and house colours throughout all the ramifications of the enterprise. Given these essentials a competent manager should be able to devise the necessary administrative rails on which the programme can run. The creation of the corporate identity is perhaps the best example of a co-operative effort between administrative and design skills from which both parties can derive equal satisfaction.

There is even a danger in this; the corporate identity can develop into an obsessive preoccupation, becoming an end in itself rather than one of the means by which the company achieves its objectives. Consequently

128

the programme needs to be constantly examined by management not only for failure to comply, but also for unnecessary elaboration or expenditure. Really effective house styles tend to be thorough, but at the same time simple and unelaborate. Frills can obscure the message as much as slovenly neglect. Although it is a difficult area for cost benefit analysis, in broad terms something of this sort has to be regularly undertaken. The scheme is a tool of the company and is something more than a toy for the design manager and the design department or a fad of the managing director. Constant review not only trims the excrescences and gingers up the laggards, it also shows where changed circumstances have made the scheme out of date or inept.

The consultant designer can with advantage be retained to survey the scheme every year or every two years and be on call to add and adapt when necessary. The manager can expect a good scheme to last in substance for about ten or fifteen years, in exceptional cases for a generation. But even the classic symbols and house styles when closely examined over a long period show subtle changes which adapt them to the operational needs and marketing requirements of the organisation. It is certainly worth arranging a review of the corporate identity schemes of leading competitors and others about every five years to assess how the company compares with the best at the time, bringing in the departments of public relations and publicity, architecture and maintenance and marketing for discussion with the designer.

The main elements should stand the company in good stead for several years and the temptation to bastardise them should be resisted, but the way they are used may well need modification. Certainly the introduction of new product plans needs careful integration in order to give full impact to the new brand and at the same time attract the prestige of the overall corporate identity. A major revision of a company's scheme should not be undertaken lightly when an identity has already been established, no matter how much a new chairman wants to establish his new style of management. But when it is done, it must be devised by professional designers backed by sophisticated management techniques. It is not an area for the enthusiastic amateur of either discipline. When there is also a sizable rebuilding programme, the architect can contribute substantially to the company's identity. The management consultant may be a preliminary to a scheme or he may be brought in as a result of a corporate identity survey.

129

Case study—BEA

It is worth looking more closely at an organisation which has successfully employed a corporate identity programme over many years and has recently revised the basic visual elements. British European Airways, BEA, has operated since the mid-forties in a climate of spectacular growth and fierce competition within international price structures which circumscribe the market activities of all airlines. Over Europe there are about forty major scheduled airlines operating between nearly all the main cities. BEA has managed to secure about a quarter of all this traffic. What the airline has to sell is a seat on an aeroplane at a particular time on a particular flight. Usually it is being offered for sale at the same price and under basically the same conditions as its competitors'. If it is not sold that slice of business is lost. Selling aircraft seats is a tough commercial challenge and BEA realised that to succeed it needed an attractive and forceful corporate identity which would appeal to customers, symbolise an efficient, safe and friendly service, and establish passenger loyalty more strongly than other airlines. BEA was among the first in the late nineteen-fifties to organise its corporate identity, appoint a design manager and introduce a design manual. The stimulus to do so came from the competitive situation in the airline business at that time.

BEA needed a corporate image which was modern. Air travel has no long history and consequently the public would regard period pastiche as inappropriate; if it was to be modern then it had to be really up to date since nothing has less appeal than last year's fashionable clichés. So it had to be modern in a fundamental enduring sense. The image also had to convey a feeling of security which is a strong subconscious need of the air traveller, and of efficiency which reinforces security and provides convenience and comfort; it had to be friendly and suggest concern for the needs of the customer. The attentiveness of the cabin staff is a major asset in selling air travel and should be used to advantage throughout the whole organisation at every point where it makes contact with the customer. The image had also to be easily recognisable and memorable if it was to be effective in the market-place.

Airlines compete on the quality of service to the customer, so the organisation's design policy can reinforce that quality and also set the standard of environment in which the staff work, of the equipment they use and of their appearance through the uniform they wear. The design manager in BEA has from the early days been concerned with all the visual aspects of the organisation in order to identify BEA as an up-to-date, safe and competent airline, market research having established clearly what characteristics the customer expects.

The customer is not just concerned with buying a ticket and then the flight. For him the actual journey may only be a focal point in a series of contacts with the airline. If he is interested in a holiday, or even a business journey, he may be planning it months ahead. He may see advertisements and then write and receive a letter enclosing leaflets which he will study. He may call several times at a sales office to make a reservation, to confirm his dates and times, and to collect and pay for his ticket and labels. He will report to the airline offices at the air terminal, meet the check-in staff, be directed by a system of notices and take an airline bus to the airport where he will again be met by staff and directed to the plane itself. Here he will be affected by the interior environment, the appearance and behaviour of the staff, the catering and the flight literature. He is similarly influenced by staff, notices and office equipment on arrival at his destination and also at the airline office abroad when he checks the details of the return journey on which he will pass through the same series of points of contact with BEA's corporate identity. From the customer's point of view the service extends over a long period often in a place which is foreign to him, where language may be unfamiliar and where there is ample opportunity for him to become confused, frustrated, lost, flustered, and even frightened. The experience of travel permits all these states of mind. Throughout the process the personality of the airline is designed to be reassuring and efficient.

As the head of BEA, Sir Anthony Millward, put it at the time:

All this goes on in a hotly competitive industry where other airlines are competing vigorously and skilfully with us for a share of the travelling public. Add to this the fact that we are selling the most perishable commodity in the word, perishable to a degree to which fish and fresh fruit (which can be kept in deep freeze) do not aspire. The airline seat perishes, if it is unsold, irrevocably the moment the aircraft door is closed and the journey begins.

The BEA programme strives to impress upon the customer at every point of contact that he is in the hands of the same efficient airline. As con-

131

sistency and coherence are the keystone, BEA management has to be continually vigilant to prevent intrusions which destroy the coherence and reduce the impact of the total effect. The tool for this is the design manual regularly revised to meet current conditions. This ensures that a professional attitude towards decisions on visual matters is adopted by senior management. Personal opinions of managers under the influence of artistic wives or aunts who are Sunday painters are kept where they belong, round the domestic hearth.

Within the organisational structure of BEA, design management has always been in the department most in contact with public attitudes, originally the advertising manager within the commercial and sales department, now the marketing organisation to which BEA believe their corporate identity contributes directly. This close association with commercial operations and advertising fosters a community of style between advertising and other visual aspects, the advertisements being the element of which the public is most constantly aware and which must therefore be in step with the design programme if a dichotomy is to be avoided. This is not to say that the advertisements dictate the image. This arrangement may well be appropriate to companies trading in the mass market and dealing in services or branded goods.

BEA are convinced that their British origin is an important element in achieving sales both in the UK and overseas. This is reflected in the new symbol designed in the late sixties by Henrion Design Associates who developed a flight symbol from the elements of the Union Jack. Both the logotype (figure 14) and the symbol emphasise the speed of the service, as an important element in the design. The development of the identity, both the one based on the red square and the new one based on the national emblem, was undertaken by both staff designers and freelance designers. Because the level of design work fluctuates according to need, and also to allow a regular injection of fresh ideas, BEA has only a nucleus of staff designers whose job is to establish the guidelines and co-ordinate the programme. At peak periods there may be up to ten freelance designers involved, graphic and industrial designers and architects. Worthwhile economies are made by expanding the team in this way only when the work load increases, as when a batch of new aircraft have to be fitted out or premises extended or refurbished, provided that the central design direction is strong and co-ordinated.

The new livery for the aircraft, vehicles and premises is designed not

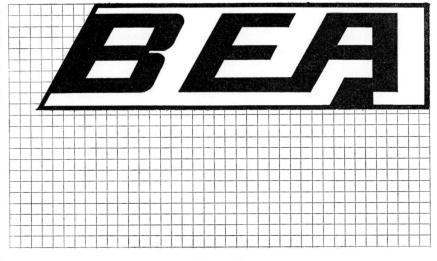

Figure 14

only to create the most favourable impression but also to achieve economy and speed in application and maintenance. Using a minimum of colours means fewer stock-holding problems, and the simple paint scheme is not only a visual advantage but is also fast to apply as it involves less masking. The high-gloss polyurethane paint chosen for the house colours has also achieved considerable reductions in air friction which saves fuel in flight. The colour for ground vehicles is chosen for its visibility in poor weather and so is a safety measure; white is used for the roofs to reduce heat absorption. The same thoroughness in reconciling the desired visual effect with function is given to the interior furnishings of the aircraft where comfort must be married with strict weight/strength ratios and fire precautions. The convenience of the passenger when eating and of the staff when storing and serving the meal is designed into trays, cups and other utensils. The same goes for the vehicles on the ground and they too carry strong identification, even to the catering vans and the aircraft servicing vehicles, so that the passenger is aware of the attention which is paid to these aspects.

133

It is also an objective of the corporate design programme to give good working conditions for the staff, as this affects customer services. Attention to the lay out of timetables and to communications equipment has achieved greater speed and accuracy. The uniform is designed to be not only smart and fashionably attractive but comfortable and practical for differing weather and duties, some of which require special protective clothing. BEA has to handle much information not only for booking and control staff who use carefully designed equipment, but also for passengers for whom a graphic system has been devised for directional signs and for displays of flight information. In these simplicity and consistency and legibility by day and night are essential to a friendly and efficient service. All documentation is subjected to the same design objectives and all BEA stationery and forms are designed to a standard for easy handling and comprehension. BEA claims that rationalisation of form design has led to vast reductions in numbers and consequently cost.

Cost is always a primary concern in such a competitive business where profitability is hard to achieve. Each design job is expected to improve the BEA service, increase efficiency and contribute to revenue; the design work is budgeted into each project and has to prove its worth either in terms of improved operation or a contribution to the image or both. Mr Henrion attributes much of the speed with which his proposals in 1967 were accepted and carried out to the high degree of design control and awareness in BEA management. By carefully planning the redesign programme it was carried through almost entirely within normal replacement and repainting cycles with over 100 aircraft, over 1000 vehicles and 183 buildings all over Europe.

The design manager supervises the programme which is defined in a two-volume design manual which details the rules for normal applications. The first volume sets out the basic elements, logotype, symbols, colours, etc., with construction drawings and details of correct usage. The second shows example of applications and illustrates how particular situations are to be dealt with, such as sales offices, print, publicity, forms, vehicles and aircraft. Consequently a signwriter abroad can produce a notice identical to its counterpart at headquarters.

When a new edition of the manual was issued Mr Henry Marking, Chairman of BEA, stressed the importance of following a clear and consistent design policy in order to present a coherent picture from every aspect. Through the wide distribution of the manual to staff who are in any way associated with the projection of the identity, a very high degree of staff involvement is assured. A fine balance needs to be maintained between enlightened flexibility and receptiveness to new ideas on the one hand and firmness in managing the operation of the programme to avoid blurring the image. As so often in management, the quality of judgement determines the difference between a silk purse and a sow's ear. Only by shrewd judgement can management keep its design programme trim and up to date, a dynamic contribution to profitability. The time will come, as it did in BEA, when corporate identity has gradually grown out of date, the climate of graphic communication has changed and the market and operational requirements are different. Management can be helped to assess this point by staff designers and particularly by the consultant designer on a retainer. By that time the organisation should be reasonably skilled in the management of a design programme, and able like BEA to plan and implement a new scheme without undue waste of time or resources.

A glance at a BEA brochure will show the scope and character of the current BEA corporate identity. It undoubtedly continues its record of efficiency and effectiveness. Much can be learnt from it and applied to parallel situations. One of the salient factors is that both the old and the new were imaginative at the time they were introduced and commanded attention. Some were even shocked at BEA's new livery, but when it was introduced it was ahead of not behind its time, and that gave it a good start for a reasonably long life. In corporate identity it pays to be at the beginning rather than the end of a tradition.

Buying policy
Another aspect of corporate identity is the buying policy of a firm for all the products which it uses itself and are evident to the customers and the staff. In a financial sense purchasing officers are normally strictly controlled, but there is often less supervision of the standards of purchases as the needs of an organisation change and grow. The system favours buying down to a price rather than to a standard. The idea of co-ordinating purchases for a recognisable design standard throughout so that everything goes with everything is not often considered as a problem of compatibility. Jasper Grindley, speaking at the time as

135

managing director of W. and A. Gilbey Limited,[1] set great store on top management controlling all buying from buildings to envelopes:

> Buyers at manager level do not yield their kingdoms easily. The normal unalienable right of a buyer is to select—and ugliness is easily purchased (often on price justification). The design director must filch these responsibilities, quietly, gradually, and firmly while at the same time educating. With luck the day will come when his advisers', his own standards and those of all key staff will, near enough fuse into one. I like to feel at Gilbey's we have reached that point. Now it is done together with a sense of common purpose. . . . I sometimes wonder whether a great wedge of the public, now walking around with their eyes fully open (particularly the young) are not well ahead of the suppliers. . . . I think there is an instinctive British resentment against help or interference in the sphere of visual judgement. Everyone is immediately an expert. And those in the highest seats are of course (with rare exceptions) the most expert. And so we continue to find the new well-designed factory producing drab articles, the new canteen spoilt by hideous notices, the designed interior made silly by unthinking later additions.

Such counsel smacks of perfection, but the principle is fundamentally right, the principle of caring about the design of everything.

The design manager may be the only responsible executive who cares enough, but like Mr Grindley he can infect his colleagues with his concern and create an atmosphere in which most people are critical of the second-rate. That does not mean that everything must be expensive and luxurious; often it is quite the reverse. The realisation that an organisation has a corporate identity, even if it is at that moment a nonentity, and that management can control and exploit its impact, can have a salutary effect on the whole apparatus of co-ordination. The design policy will set a standard for a great number of the items which accompany purchases and will take into account the relationship which exists between them. Purchasing lists will not be seen just as an array of isolated goods, but as components in a system of achieving company objectives. The emphasis may shift from buying in isolation largely on price, to buying on value and on the contribution made to the system as

[1] Now International Distillers and Vintners.

a whole. Americans are apt to talk about total design when they wish to stress the interdependence of the design of the exterior of a building and the interior, the design of letterheads and the machines and skills in the typing pool, the design of products and packaging and publicity, the design of air-conditioning and uniforms and clothing.

For a long time the design skills in transport concentrated on the propulsion of the train, the ship or the coach. Passenger comfort was at best acknowledged by decorative frills. In the total design concept a railway undertaking would not only, at the appropriate moment, redesign the locomotives and the carriages but also the seating, the furnishings, the colour schemes, the communications systems, the graphics, the advertising and the publicity, all in a properly phased and budgeted programme. This does not mean in an office that all the office furniture has to be specially designed if the firm moves into new accommodation, but it does mean that the purchasing officer will have a broad specification which embraces design standards and against which he will review what is offered on the market. For reasonably large orders the supplier will probably be prepared to make marginal modifications to bring the product into line with a customer's requirements. The enlightened manufacturer will welcome this approach, provided it is amicable to his production programme, because it can inject improvements into his range of products which are welcomed by other customers. Development costs for new designs are usually a headache to the manufacturer and it can be an advantage to have a progressive client with whom to share the costs (see Race case study on p. 149). Some managements whose design departments have worked out a new design to be produced for their use by a manufacturer press for control of the copyright. There is some sense in this but the manager also has to appreciate the manufacturer's problems and give him the chance to recoup part of his development cost through other customers. This should also reduce the cost to the originator. It is not difficult to negotiate an agreement which meets both points of view. The originator will get some credit for his design leadership and his name may be attached to the product as in the case of the dining-chair made by Race Furniture Limited for the new Cunarder *QE 2*.

Mr Leslie Julius of the furniture firm of Hille, believes that the contribution of the corporate customer is of the utmost importance to the manufacturer. Each customer has his own specific requirements which can be fulfilled by the manufacturer working in close co-operation with him and the designer. In many instances the designer can so cope with these requirements as to make the end product suitable for other markets and other customers. Mr Julius found this to be so with the furniture he made for Gatwick Airport to the designs of Robin Day; the furniture, because of its special aesthetic and functional qualities, satisfied many other people's needs. Gatwick itself was initially an example of every object down to the last detail being thought through and carefully designed.

The manager with a fully developed design policy can, therefore, seek out progressive manufacturers who will be prepared to undertake with him designs to meet his requirements and relate them to his market. Such a relationship often results in a product which not only has a high functional and aesthetic standard but also meets the requirements of maintenance more effectively. This is of great importance, for example, in the case of a dining-chair for a hotel dining-room. The chair must not only be designed to be comfortable for the guest (but not too comfortable so that he stays too long), convenient for the waiter and the cleaning staff, but it also must be durable and constantly smart and clean looking. If an average of five chairs in a hundred have to be withdrawn for repair at any one time, replacement chairs have to be bought and stored, because the restaurant cannot be without them. Added to this, the repair bills have to be paid, so the management will probably be well advised to put more money into design and initial cost to avoid the extra purchase and maintenance cost and attendant waste of administrative time.

A design manager will make sure that the design policy covers bulk purchasing and that there is contact between purchasing officers and designers where expensive manufactured products are concerned. This will gradually help the buyers to sharpen their analytical approach to products and assess more accurately whether what they are buying has the right design characteristics for the job. A design policy not only covers what a company produces, it covers also what it buys, and the two together, properly co-ordinated, contribute to the corporate identity. Too few managers use their power as corporate customers to force the pace of design development.

Case study—Sainsbury

J. Sainsbury and Co. Limited, although essentially different from BEA in origins and operations, arrived at a strong corporate identity through a climate of strong competition. Originally a dairy in Covent Garden, Sainsbury expanded in London and then in the provinces. The stimulus for the corporate identity came from the need to standardise, first the shop front then the window display and eventually the style of the shop itself, the posters and the showcards. This meant refusing the advertising material offered by manufacturers. Standardisation of fittings, fixtures, tiles, floors and woodwork made the planning, building and fitting both faster and cheaper. Window displays were designed centrally and plans sent to branches. Much of the standardisation was for functional as well as aesthetic reasons, so that surfaces could be easily cleaned and dirt and grease traps avoided. The elimination of fussy detail enhanced rather than reduced the recognition impact. The personality which Sainsbury's wanted to portray was one of honest fair trading, good quality and cleanliness which is a vital asset to the food trade.

In the early fifties a store outside London was converted partially into self-service although many foods were still rationed. This proved that the pattern of retailing was about to change rapidly. At that time the fittings had to be purpose-made, even the refrigeration cabinets, and this helped to contribute to the personality of the stores which were often architecturally very different. Eventually a compromise due to the need to reconcile cost and design requirements was reached by accepting a fundamentally standard unit based to some extent on past experience, slightly modified and finished in Sainsbury colours. The planning of the shop conformed with the character of the corporate identity by having wide aisles uncluttered by display and all the shop dressing giving an impression of orderliness. This restrained approach to the shop itself allowed the goods on the shelves to provide the colour. In the mid-sixties Sainsbury had between four hundred and five hundred brand lines extending into the non-food range. The design of the packaging was carefully contrived to emphasise quality and clean straightforward trading. Information was limited to the basic essentials, the printing clear and the type plain, weight and price being shown boldly on the front. The total impact on the customer was effective both in the shop and later at home on the customer's shelves.

139

The Sainsbury logotype (facing p. 97) is now standardised on the fascias. At one time the typeface was a classic roman based on the Trajan column, but although this looked distinguished it was not easy to read at an angle which is often the most frequent view the shopper has of the fascia. So it was later changed to Albertus, the typeface which their design consultant Leonard Beaumont was then using on the company's packaging. This was eventually dropped in favour of Venus by Peter Dixon who became Chief Designer after Mr Beaumont retired. All point-of-sale material is designed by the staff designers to conform with the house style under the direction of the chief designer. The design studio under Peter Dixon works side by side with the advertising department both being immediately responsible to the Chairman, John Sainsbury. The whole corporate image was controlled through a weekly meeting of the chairman, the advertising manager with his assistant and the chief designer when briefs for new work were agreed and design work progressed. This tight organisation allowed free discussion of all problems, giving the designer the opportunity to explain the reasons for his proposals. This procedure avoided the less direct method of going through an advertising agent. The close relationship eliminates misunderstandings and gives the designer the necessary involvement with top management and the overall policy of the company. Mr John Sainsbury summed this up:

I believe—and I know that I am not alone in this view—that one should look at these problems of design not as individual items but how each fits in with the other in the wider sense. However good a single item may be, its importance and value is lost, or at any rate diminished, if it is not related to the whole. If careful attention is paid to the way in which each individual item—the shop front, interior decor, design of fittings, packaging, display material—fits into the whole, then providing each is well and tastefully produced, the overall effect and impact can be tremendous. We count ourselves fortunate in my company that we can bring all these things together and in doing so, we hope that we are not only doing ourselves a service, but also providing pleasant and attractive conditions for the housewife to shop in.

The success of this dual service is reflected in the profitability of the Sainsbury enterprise and provides a good example of the skilful management of design services in a firm in the retail trade.

Chapter 5

Design Case Studies

British Thornton

British Thornton, manufacturers of slide-rules and drawing instruments, provides one of the best examples of a firm which ran into difficulties in the 1950s because market conditions changed, cost of labour rose and the design of their products was related to techniques of manufacture and packaging which had become unprofitable. Fortunately, senior management recognised that their problem was basically one of relating design to current user requirements and new production methods.

Product policy
Since the 1920s Thornton had made as a major part of their production a range of thirty-four slide-rules of three different lengths with a wide variety of scale combinations. They were made by traditional processes of cutting blanks from selected mahogany which were then left to season for several months. These were then shaped into rules by a series of careful machine operations and the necessary grooves made. Tension springs were fitted, six to each slide-rule, and then the slides were fitted. The rules were laminated with white celluloid sheet on the face and edges and faced up by another machining operation. When the celluloid face had been carefully divided and the figures pressed in, the blank divisions and figures were filled with red or black and sandpapered by hand to remove burrs. The slides had then to be hand worked to give them the correct degree of even friction. Finally the rules were cleaned up and the cursors fitted. Thus the design programme for each slide-rule required the manufacture of twenty-three separate parts, not counting the cursors. The slide-rules were excellent, but they had to be made in batches using about 75 per cent skilled male labour with a large amount of hand work and 25 per cent semi-skilled labour.

The attitude of Thornton to the cases for their drawing instruments was similar. For years the instruments were stored in velvet lined cases with individual recesses for the various pieces, different sets of instruments being offered, each in a different size of case with appropriate recesses. This variety of combinations entailed production in small batches largely by hand. The wooden cases were covered in leather cloth with the interior recesses cut out and lined with velvet; finally metal hinges and clasps were attached by hand. The cases were handsome but the hand work and the length of the production time made them uneconomic, and in use the leather cloth became scuffed and the velvet lining could become dirty and faded.

During the fifties the firm's managing director, Mr R. T. Reynolds, realised that the existing designs involved too much skilled hand work to be economic, that the diversity of the ranges must be reduced in order to rationalise production, even if this meant a marginal restriction of the width of their market, and that this loss of custom should be compensated by selling to overseas markets. As Mr Reynolds explained to an export conference: 'Design flexibility involves thinking and operating in terms of an international market as distinct from a national one. We want to keep modification of our products to a minimum, so that there is a minimum interference with production schedules and we keep our prices at the lowest possible level and give good delivery.' Thus he emphasised, 'the design policy is to concentrate energies and expertise in the manufacture of a rationalised range of functionally designed products of high quality standards. The aim is to compete on design as distinct from price and to give optimum value for money.'

Research

In 1960 British Thornton, then a small limited company with 220 employees, decided to introduce their new product policy by undertaking a thorough design reorganisation. As a first step management asked the Design Council to recommend a designer or a design team who might carry out what they described at the time as a 'corporate identity programme'. Several names were put forward and after discussions and interviews the design consultants, Stevenson-Ward of Macclesfield, were appointed for a trial period of one year; at the time of writing they are still Thornton's consultant designers.

British Thornton's principal markets were defined in the field of education, distribution being through local education authorities, book-stores in colleges as well as through the retail trade. In the case of slide-rules it was not thought practicable to manufacture and market econo-mically the wide range which would be involved if all possible scale combinations were offered. The market was therefore divided into five principal groups: the professional user and student requiring a wide computation field; the general-purpose user who desires trigono-metrical and log–log scales; the general-purpose user, who does not require trigonometrical and log–log scales; school users requiring trigo-nometrical and log–log scales; and school users not requiring these.

A high degree of accuracy was considered an essential characteristic for this market. Research proved that only a homogeneous material with minimum stress would give the requisite standard of accuracy, any form of laminated construction being of questionable stability. After exhaustive tests the design team decided to use an injection-moulded body for the slide-rules in a very stable material which would not vary in different climates.

It was established that the required degree of accuracy could only be guaranteed if the two stocks of a slide-rule are held positively in relation to each other, and the designers were asked to incorporate this require-ment in their basic solution rather than provide a secondary means of securing the stocks as this would involve the user in making an adjust-ment. Thornton were aware that inaccuracy in reading in the double faced type of slide rule can be caused by lateral pressure across the rule and the designers investigated how to avoid this.

Market research showed that a satisfactory market did exist although Thornton at the time had only a small share of it, despite their good reputation. Careful investigation further showed that it was possible to rationalise the thirty-four models down to five and still meet the needs of the majority of customers; also, a length of 250 mm could be used for all the rules. Users learn how to operate slide-rules when carrying out calcu-lations on the basic scales which apply to all slide-rules. This is quickly learnt with a little practice and the application of the more advanced scales depends largely on the mathematical knowledge of the user. So detailed instructions were devoted to the basic scales. Market research confirmed that slide-rules were very often carried by the user, so the pack had to be both durable and convenient. As part of the long-term appraisal of the company's products the range of instruments was

143

reviewed in the light of changes in the educational and professional fields. Traditionally the multi-purpose instrument was regarded as the basic instrument for technical drawings. The compass half set was in almost universal use with its various attachments and spring bows and beam compasses. The appraisal concluded that the multi-purpose instrument is unsound in principle and play developing through the joints causes a loss of accuracy; that teachers of technical drawing seem to prefer to encourage the use of pencil instruments only; that the need for ink has been reduced by the increased use of reprographic processes. Consequently it was suggested that, as pen-compasses were costly to produce and used infrequently, they were less economic. The important factor was to produce instruments of first-rate design with which high standards of functional efficiency satisfaction could be achieved by both educational and professional users. So the product policy was to market instruments of this high standard of accuracy and performance which can only be obtained by designing each instrument to carry out one function as perfectly as possible. One instrument for one job was the principle whenever practicable. It was, however, realised that this concept would not be immediately accepted by the market, so that the traditional type of instrument would continue as alternatives where appropriate.

For the design of ruling pens it was decided that optimum accuracy should have priority over ease of cleaning and this led to the adoption of the fixed nib throughout. For the finish of the instruments Thornton required high resistance to tarnish and corrosion, freedom from internal stress without peeling or flaking, hard and durable and attractive appearance. A stainless finish, tin-nickel alloy electroplating, which had already been proved by the company, was entirely suitable.

Thornton attached great importance to its packaging policy, believing that instruments of such high quality deserved good protection and presentation and maximum convenience for the user. As the traditional wooden cases with their individual recesses were too costly, inflexible in layout, and cumbersome, their form and method of manufacture were completely reassessed. With the rigid interior layout of the old cases, the user, faced with the problem of deciding what combination of instruments to buy, had to choose either a full set for present and future needs some of which he might never in fact use, or a smaller set containing only those items required at the time, but running the risk of requiring

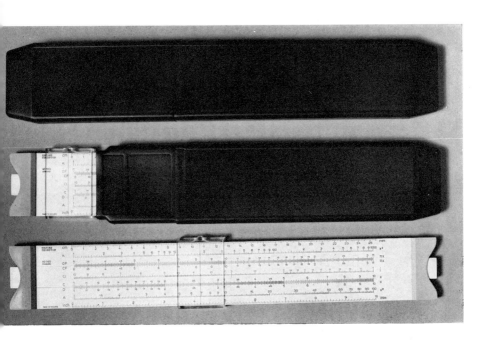

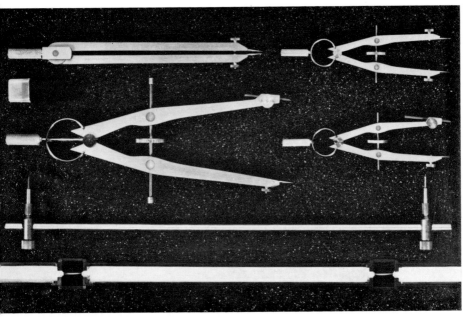

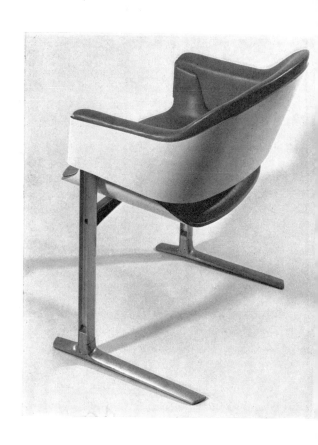

additional instruments later which the case would not accommodate. It was therefore essential for the designers to find a flexible solution, capable of economic production.

Brief

These investigations and a series of meetings between management and designers resulted in a clear design brief to produce a range of slide-rules and instruments suitable for educational and professional use, rationalising the number of existing models to achieve considerable variety reduction. The products should be suitable for selling in most climates throughout the world. High quality, accurate and convenient performance and clear legibility were given priority. The slide-rules should give answers to an accuracy of three significant figures which is adequate for most calculations and is therefore the required limit of accuracy. Instructions would concentrate on basic scales and the finish for the instruments should be trouble free. The case for the drawing instruments should be convenient for carrying, afford sound protection with better cleanliness and allow the user to put into them his own choice of pieces and add to them without difficulty. The whole product range should be designed to take advantage of labour-saving techniques and materials and be suitable for quantity production. Finally the range should be presented to the market within a strong corporate identity including the company's print based on international paper sizes, packaging, publicity and architecture. As this was a new venture as far as Thornton was concerned the management relied on their consultant designers to interpret these requirements, to put forward their own suggestions and to formulate their programme.

Design work

As the management's approach was to achieve a thorough overhaul of the company's activities the programme extended over some seven years and involved the introduction of new machinery and manufacturing techniques as well as some retraining.

For the slide-rules the basic range was reduced to five then four models covering the majority of users, incorporating the differential scales which enable the user to carry out a wider and more comprehensive range of computations, maintaining consistently high accuracy, and providing sine and tangent range to zero angle. The designers were

145

remarkably successful in reconciling the apparently conflicting requirements of high quality and efficiency with economic manufacture. They departed from the traditional methods described by adopting the injection-moulding process for the stocks and slides using an ABS thermoplastics material which is suitably stable, being virtually immune from variations in any climatic conditions likely to be encountered in overseas markets, with freedom from embrittlement and high resistance to wear and tear and discoloration which would affect legibility. By the adoption of end caps it was possible to avoid lateral pressure across the width which disturbs accuracy. These end caps are assembled on the stocks by mortice and tenon joint and bonded securely together. When the slide lies between the stocks the rule is held by the end caps and the slide manipulated by the index finger. When the slide extends beyond the stocks the rule is held by one end cap and the slide manipulated by the free hand. Any pressure across the width of the rule is thus avoided and accuracy is ensured. The precision of the assembly permits the required degree of friction between slide and stocks, giving a permanently smooth and even movement of the slide. The end caps allow the slide rule to be used on a flat working surface by leaving the slide free to move and they also protect the scales from abrasion. A degree of spring tension is applied in manufacture to avoid the need for adjustment but does not interfere with the evenness of movement. The risk of wear and tear in use is minimised by the injection-moulded skins on the bearing surfaces of the two stocks and the slide (facing p. 144).

The designers arranged the scales to give logical presentation and easy identification; the more specialised scales were dissociated from the fundamental scales whenever practicable, red figures being used to indicate scales which run in the reverse direction. For maximum comfort to the eyes a matt surface was used to avoid reflections. The characters were selected to give legibility in the smallest size. By using a three-point location the cursor gives a positive seating on the datum face and correct alignment of the hair line.

To protect the rule the case was designed in blow-moulded polythene with a pull off cap, and it is therefore virtually indestructible in the conditions in which it is likely to be used. The case is then inserted into a carton carrying the company's logotype and house style.

For the drawing instruments the designers accepted the policy of one instrument one job, based on the analysis that multi-purpose instruments do not give maximum efficiency in use. Where radius of circle is concerned the instruments were divided into three groups, up to 40 mm radius, up to 125 mm and over 125 mm, the radius up to 125 mm being the most important. The 125 mm pencil compass is therefore the most useful single instrument. This had to be of outstanding rigidity so that the pencil drawings, made with adequate pressure to give good line density, can be used for reprographic purposes. The pencil compass was, therefore, designed with solid legs free from any weaknesses from joints, with centre screw adjustment for accurate setting and using nylon bearings for smooth and even movement so that it should have both rigidity and convenience.

The divider and pen compass need no pressure and were designed with a ball bearing self-centring head incorporating thrust washers to retain its setting. No further setting device for fine adjustment was needed. For a radius over 125 mm the beam compass was found to give the highest accuracy: it has moveable heads and is converted to a divider by substituting a needle point for the pencil lead. All fittings such as needles, nuts, bolts, etc., were examined in order to achieve standardisation as far as practicable and a visual relationship where appropriate. For the surface the stainless steel finish met all requirements.

The designers had decided that the cases would be strong, light and economical if they were injection-moulded thermoplastics but this would be expensive if each set had different interior mouldings into which the appropriate instruments were slotted. The necessity for these separate compartments was avoided by designing the interior without separations and fitting resilient pressure pads of polyurethane of the correct density in both lid and base, so that the instruments selected by the user to suit his personal requirements could be firmly secured (see plate III, facing p. 144). When the case is closed the pressure pads sandwich the instruments and hold them in a resilient grip which protects them far better than the old velvet lined recesses. This method allows different numbers and types of instrument to be accommodated in the same case which was then freed from the previous limitation of variety and sizes. Consequently it was possible to develop one case for all combinations and the much larger quantities required could be injection moulded in ABS with integrally moulded clasps and robust polypropylene hinges slotted into specially moulded cavities. Both lid and base were moulded in the same tool. The plastic hinges were simply pushed into the moulded recesses in

147

the lid and base to connect the two parts. The only other operation was to insert the foam pressure pads and put the completed case into its outer carton.

Results

The new design of the cases gave the company a reduction in manufacturing cost and a great saving in the cost of factory storage because formerly a large stock of various sizes had to be held against customer demand. The space previously used by the case department could be put to other uses. The new case also gave much better functional efficiency and suited the majority of users, being stronger, easier to keep clean and giving better protection to the instruments. The customer could now buy a case to contain the instruments that he currently needed and be able to add more as required, without any difficulty of fitting them into the case.

The company claims that the other tangible results of the scheme were increased sales and further reductions in costs which were directly attributable to the design programme. Sales of drawing instruments rose by 44 per cent, costs were reduced by 15 per cent and the number of different instruments produced was reduced by 30 per cent. Sales of instrument cases were increased by 37 per cent, costs were reduced by 15 per cent and the number and types were reduced by 30 per cent. The thirty-four different slide-rules produced in 1960 were reduced to four with a 48 per cent increase in sales and a 40 per cent reduction in costs.

The designers have succeeded in the difficult task of improving the products and at the same time reducing manufacturing costs. As a result British Thornton say it has consolidated its position in a highly competitive market, with a progressive increase in profits. It is also now well adapted from a management point of view to take advantage of new changes in materials and production techniques. Dealing with designers has injected an attitude of innovation into the firm's management style which is an asset of considerable long-term benefit. Thornton were fortunate in being small enough to change without critical disruption, in having a flexible and imaginative management, and in choosing talented and trustworthy designers, and being prepared to trust them. It may also have been a case of do or die and that alone simplifies the decisions.

Race Furniture

The history of Race Furniture is rather different from British Thornton in that the former began only in 1945 and both the Managing Director, Noel Jordan, and Ernest Race, Director of Design, were motivated by a consuming interest in engineering research, development and design. Although they shared a shrewd business sense and maintained a viable enterprise over twenty-five years, their main satisfaction derived from the neat and elegant solution of design problems, believing that if they produced furniture of the highest quality there would be a limited but profitable market. On that basis they determined to stay in business and have done so despite their unconventional attitude.

Product Policy—BA Chair

In the nineteen-thirties Noel Jordan ran an engineering firm, Enness Sentinel Limited, making a variety of products ranging from precision tools to heavy prefabricated davits for ships' lifeboats. Its skills and resources were then devoted to the war effort and the firm became involved in many engineering products including the development of floats for the Mulberry invasion harbour. In 1945 this work came to an end and Noel Jordan had the opportunity of gaining control of the firm by acquiring the majority shareholding. He had always been interested in the work of the Bauhaus in Germany in the thirties and he now believed that its experiments in metal furniture provided a basis for applying engineering techniques in the furniture industry which at that time relied almost entirely on craft traditions. He realised that there was a prejudice in the market against metal furniture because older people thought it clinical and unsympathetic. On the other hand a new generation was returning from the war familiar with machines and appreciative of engineering skills. Jordan decided that there was a limited but expanding market for furniture designed to exploit the qualities of fine engineering.

The difficulties were formidable. Licences for timber and textiles were only available to firms already in business. The type of furniture proposed did not come within the utility specifications and consequently attracted purchase tax up to 66 per cent. Shortages of all kinds confronted such an enterprise. But Jordan knew that there was a supply of surplus aluminium available without licence which might give him a

149

starting-point. His assets at that time were a factory, his own engineering knowledge, a source of supply and a hunch that a new type of furniture would be acceptable to the post-war generation. Knowing that the key to the success of the project depended on design ability he advertised for a designer. He simply stated that an engineering firm would like to receive applications from a designer who believed that an engineering approach was appropriate to the manufacture of modern furniture. As he sorted the replies Noel Jordan searched for clues to creativity first and then a sympathetic personality with whom he could work. Among the applicants was Ernest Race who had some architectural training, a little experience in designing light fittings in the design studio at Troughton and Young and also in textiles. For a short time he had run a small shop in Knightsbridge. In the interview Race gave ample evidence that he was highly creative and Jordan immediately felt that he could work with him. So he offered him the job. Race rapidly demonstrated his thorough approach to design problems, his appreciation of engineering techniques, his analytical mind, his creativity and his ability to get on with Jordan. Race was not prolific but he was very thoughtful, carefully working out each idea and weeding out those that were unsatisfactory. Before he reached a decision he might scrap hundreds of ideas, but once he was convinced that he had the right answer he was difficult to shift, although he would always listen to Jordan's views on engineering and production techniques. Jordan realised that he had an outstanding designer in Ernest Race and was anxious to secure his services on a permanent basis. So he formed a subsidiary to Enness Sentinel, Ernest Race Limited (now Race Furniture Limited) with himself as managing director with a majority shareholding and Ernest Race as design director. As the firm developed Race showed that he was extremely price conscious. If initially an item worked out at £20 he would work assiduously to bring it down to £19. Economy of means became a typical aspect of Race Furniture.

Research
Race explored and exploited the available materials, and as Noel Jordan records, revealed an uncanny sense of what could be achieved by developing new manufacturing techniques and using materials in a way that they had never been used before. This brought a sense of challenge to all the technicians who worked with him. During the development of a

150

design, much of the work related to straightforward physical research in which Race was adept at fusing the different skills of art and science.

Race accepted that initially the frame of the BA chair would have to be made by sand-casting which produces a rough texture requiring much finishing and polishing with mops revolving at high speed in order to make it visually acceptable. He therefore experimented with shapes that would allow the visible surfaces to be finished and polished flat with the minimum of skill on the part of the operator. He decided that a T-section would be the most suitable. In order to save weight and cost and create an instant visual effect he decided that the T-section should be tapered. He then had to eliminate all abrupt changes in section where there was a concentration of stress which could result in fracture. By gradually eliminating all sharp corners Race minimised the difficulties of the foundry and because production could be quicker and less castings were rejected, he reduced cost.

The construction and upholstery of the seat and backrest could not be solved conventionally because there was no licence for wood or fabrics. Race experimented with a flock spraying technique but this failed because plywood could not be used as the base. Some white ex-RAF cotton duck was found and piece-dyed, and rubberised hair was used as cushion material. At first the castings were finished off with wax but eventually a stove enamel process was used which was more efficient and economical.

When the original chair was shown at the 'Britain Can Make It' Exhibition at the Victoria and Albert Museum in 1946, it was seen by the managing director of a foundry who was interested in the technique of die-casting which had been developed to produce millions of incendiary bomb casings during the war. Tests were carried out to discover whether the long tapered leg components could be successfully die-cast. The results showed that this was not only possible but also achieved greater strength by improving the grain flow in the metal. Studies of the chair and its structure led to the reduction of its total weight to 7 pounds 10 ounces which was a saving of about 25 per cent from the weight of the sand-castings. This discovery not only produced a stronger chair but it was visually more attractive, being more slender, and finishing was simplified by the greater accuracy of the pressure die-casting. Thus this design revision achieved a substantial reduction in the number of machining operations required and assembly was made easier; the factory cost of the chair was almost halved.

151

Brief

Race's brief evolved through discussions and trials as is often the case, rather than being clearly and completely stated at the beginning. This was acceptable because the firm was small and the managing director and the design director shared a close mutual understanding. In a large firm it would have been much more important to set out the requirements and the resources in detail at the start. The task, as it emerged, was to design an all-purpose upright chair for use in offices and canteens, using advanced engineering techniques to achieve a high standard of quality. Every opportunity was to be taken to reduce the cost, consistent with quality, and the chair was to be strong, elegant and modern in style.

It would be designed to make use of resmelted aluminium alloy from wartime products such as aircraft, and sand-casting of a tapered T-section used for the components of the chair's frame; this was later revised in favour of low-pressure die-casting, probably the first use of the method for a commercial product. Finishing processes were to be reduced as much as possible, preferably to be carried out by unskilled operatives. White cotton duck to be dyed to a suitable range of colours was to be used for the covering and rubberised hair for the filling. Strength, lightness and serviceability as well as fine appearance were to be the characteristics on which the chair would sell. The distorted conditions of the time prevented any thorough market research into how and to whom such a chair would be sold; at the time the only tangible justification was the confidence of the managing director who believed that the market was ready for qualities of this kind.

Design work

Race had settled the boundaries of the design problem in the research stage when he was experimenting with the form of metal sections, methods of finishing and upholstery. By a process of rejection and refinement he had established the broad outlines of the design. The research and development had given him a clear idea of the appearance of the chair and within this overall conception he set to work to solve the subsidiary problems. He realised, however, that the quality of the finished chair depended upon the accurate detailing of every part in order to reconcile both technical and aesthetic requirements. In this respect a high degree of accuracy was needed because the components of the chair were to be made in different places and had to fit together exactly at the point of assembly. The cast aluminium components were made in a foundry, the steel studs by a firm in the Midlands and the sewn cotton duck came from an upholstery firm in London. All these separate items were designed with a common relationship and their dimensions strictly controlled from every aspect. So thorough were Race's researching and testing that as soon as he had gone firm on the optimum solution and agreed it with Jordan, who kept in close touch with each development, he moved rapidly towards the final specification and the production models. He was not, however, prone to absolutism, and faced with the possibility of improving the performance, appearance and manufacturing techniques by the die-casting method which was suggested when the chair was first shown to the public, Race pursued the modification with enthusiasm. Jordan too was a perfectionist but he also saw in the proposed modification the realisation of his basic idea expressed in the product policy, namely to use precision engineering to produce sophisticated furniture at reasonable cost.

Such a fundamental change in production technique at so late a stage inevitably created difficult management decisions, but the improvement was directly in line with what the firm was setting out to do. It fitted perfectly with the company's objectives and Jordan decided that the long-term advantages would justify the delay in quantity production. In such a situation many managements might have hesitated, believing the more elegant design to be only a marginal asset, although the cost-reduction factor would undoubtedly be attractive. Race and Jordan had no doubts, and the second stage of the design work was expeditiously put in hand. Years later a method of photo-analysis was developed which showed behaviour of metal structures under stress. Race's calculations were proved by this method to be both economical and effective.

Jordan applied the logic of his engineering approach to the presentation of the chair to the market. The refined characteristics of the chair made an instant appeal to architects and designers. It was of considerable interest to the designers at the 'Britain Can Make It' exhibition when the chair was first shown and they placed one of the first orders for a batch to be used in the catering area of the exhibition. This indicated the kind of professional customer to whom the chair would appeal, and the form of presentation for the chair which Jordan and Race were

153

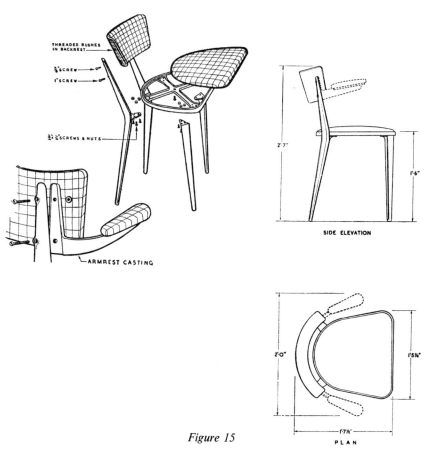

THREADED BUSHES
IN BACKREST

½"SCREW

1"SCREW

2½ 2"SCREWS & NUTS

ARMREST CASTING

SIDE ELEVATION

2'7"

1'6"

PLAN

2'0"

1'5¼"

1'7½"

Figure 15

evolving was designed to suit the professional buyer who is more objective in his criteria than the retail trade.

In the first instance the design effort for promotional material went into first-rate photographs of the product which could be given to potential customers with a factual explanation of the structural and performance characteristics of the chair. This approach gradually led to the designing of a catalogue remarkable at the time. It was akin to the high-quality literature designed for architects to illustrate building components. The designer's sketches were used to show the basic features of the chair such as junctions and other constructional details, together with measured drawings showing the side elevations and the plans (figure 15). On the opposite page there was a photograph of an

154

interior showing the chairs in use. Under the designer's sketches the entry for the BA chair read:

Idea behind the design. By using light alloy cast metal components an all-purpose upright chair has been produced which is virtually everlasting; which for transport over long distance or for export can be supplied in knock down state and easily assembled at destination by unskilled labour; it is equally suitable for any climatic conditions. By the use of upholstered seat and back the coldness often associated with metal furniture has been eliminated. Materials and construction: legs and seat frame are of die cast aluminium alloy. The seat consists of a specially moulded foam rubber cushion on a plywood base which is screwed to the metal frame. The back rest is padded and is of formed plywood. Each leg is fastened to the seat frame by three bolts. Antinoise leather inserts can be put into the bottom of each leg under certain circumstances. For re-covering in a small patterned or plain material half a yard by 48 inches or one yard by 36 inches is required. Finishes: metal components: cream-grey or satin-aluminium stove enamel. Seat and back: covering fabric of the purchaser's choice.

There was almost a complete absence of emotive blurb, indicating that it was for a professional audience. The drawings were printed on different coloured backgrounds to indicate different ranges of furniture. The design orientation of the company was emphasised by the credits not only to the designer of the furniture but also to the photographer and to the print designer which, twenty years ago, was not common practice. This catalogue consisted of loose leaves and was unusual because the covers and leaves were secured by two elastic bands held by notches on the spine. From this a number of smaller leaflets giving thumbnail photographs of the range of furniture with informative detail were printed. The design of the print was as advanced for the time as the chair.

Results

The amount of design development put into the BA chair was fully justified. The company claims that it has been the most successful design in its range. It has already a life of twenty-five years and over a quarter of a million have been made using 850 tons of aluminium in their manufacture which can, when the chairs are no longer required, be resmelted with small loss and reused. It has been marketed and assembled by unskilled labour in many countries throughout the world. It has won for the company an international reputation for advanced modern design and quality. It was frequently specified by designers as an accessory for exhibitions and interior schemes. This prestige through exhibitions made it well known among architects and professional buyers, so that it became a contract rather than a retail item, although in the early days most of the leading retail shops in England did order it. One of the first sizable orders came from BEA which itself was a pace setter in design. In retrospect it is clear that the original product policy and the professional rather than commercial attitude of the management and design director defined a chair for the contract market where buying is based on professional assessments. The company's concentration on the professional interest which the chair created, rather than the shop outlets, proved correct in this instance and set the marketing pattern for the firm's future. They had not made the mistake of selling the right product to the wrong market. The chair's success also confirmed the management's conviction that design innovation could be profitable if carried out thoroughly and logically, marrying advanced techniques with forward-looking aesthetics.

Product Policy—QE 2 Chair
From 1945 to 1969 Race Furniture designed ranges of distinguished furniture many of which sold profitably in the contract market, some receiving awards for their design merit. The firm had an established reputation for design development to meet the specialised requirements of the contract customer. It was to be expected, therefore, that when the design team for the new Cunarder, *QE 2*, needed dining-chairs for the first-class and tourist restaurants, they should approach Race Furniture.

Unfortunately, Ernest Race had died some years before, but since then Noel Jordan had worked with both young and mature designers. When the opportunity to submit a design for the *QE* chair occurred, Jordan decided that the furniture designer, Robert Heritage, had the qualities and experience to devise a solution worthy of the challenge. Jordan's thoughts turned to the success of the BA chair designed twenty-four years before as an indestructible and elegant chair for public use. Heritage had also designed dining-chairs using aluminium alloy but employing different manufacturing techniques; he, like Race, was

156

vitally interested in new materials and methods and also like Race, he had a thrusting intellect which challenged the technical people concerned with the development and manufacture of his designs.

Market research had shown that no suitable restaurant chair for the *QE 2* existed in the United Kingdom. When Jordan was approached by Cunard's designers, he immediately saw from past experience an opportunity to carry out design research and development with an enlightened client. Such opportunities are rare, but with the right management and design skills can provide a basis for the development of a range of products which do not yet exist, and can be suitable for a wider contract market than the original order. As part of the firm's product policy, Jordan sought corporate customers with whom he could share the development costs of new designs. Cunard's enquiry was exactly in line with this policy. Restaurant chairs usually fail to measure up to the exacting requirements of public use; they need to be strong so that they do not constantly have to be repaired and replaced, they must be comfortable for eating and conversation, convenient for the waiter when seating guests and serving food, easy to keep smart and clean, light to move across pile carpet and able to withstand the onslaughts of ham-fisted cleaners and porters, as well as the weight and sudden movements of well-fed clients. The BA chair had been painstakingly designed in vacuo; Cunard offered the chance to develop a luxury and a utilitarian chair combining Cunard's knowledge of user requirements with Race's skill in design development.

Research
The user requirements for smart appearance without a forest of legs in the restaurant, for durability and convenience in use and upkeep (any maintenance should be completed by normal tradesmen in the short turn-round in port) were set out by Cunard's catering staff; moreover, the chairs had to be fireproof or fire resistant. Heritage immediately carried out a number of experiments in his workshop, making a series of models whose precision impressed the works staff. He envisaged a chair supported on two legs with alternative seat and backrests for the two restaurants. The leg could be die-cast in aluminium alloy and the foot would have to be carefully designed to give sufficient stability and the junction between foot and leg would have to stand up to considerable stress. Heritage first considered fixing the foot to the leg by welding,

157

riveting or using a stainless steel screw, but when the first foot casting and the extrusion were brought together, it was found that a fail-safe joint could be designed by bonding the extrusion because the stressed areas would be sheer. Such a joint would simplify the machining operations needed on the side members of the die-casting. Experimental work was, therefore, carried out to secure the right structure for the joint and the right adhesive material.

The test procedure assessed the loading on the joint per square inch of area in sheer. This calculation gave a theoretical load of 166 lbs. which was increased arbitrarily to 600 lbs. per square inch. Two pieces of aluminium alloy were then glued together, giving a butted area of one square inch, and tested out of doors in a rig loaded with 600 lbs. of iron castings. At intervals during twelve months of testing, the sample was baked for twenty-five minutes at 450° Fahrenheit, immersed in boiling water for ten minutes and again placed on the exposure testing rig with the 600 lbs. load to stress the adjacent faces of the glue line far beyond the thermal and humidity conditions they would receive in service. The adhesive withstood these tests without failure.

On the basis that pre-formed plywood shells and liners would be used for the shaped seats and backs the company found that the back shell required manufacturing techniques entirely different from those previously used. The proposed conical shape of the back involved modifying existing plant, introducing special cutters and training skilled operators. Special post-forming jigs and heaters had to be designed and manufactured to make the right radius of the shells from the return bends (see facing p. 145). Research was also needed to discover the best method of moulding the special polythene cushions which Heritage had in mind, and despite the unusualness of the design Dunlop's technical staff eventually found a moulding method which was completely successful. As the conception of the product developed Heritage found that in order to reach the optimum solution he had to draw on the specialised knowledge of a wide range of experts.

The Brief

The brief which eventually emerged was to design two dining-chairs, one for the first-class and one for the tourist restaurant, differentiated for the two areas by alternative treatments of the upholstery. The main structure of the two chairs would be identical to achieve economies in the cost of dies, machining fixtures and toolings. The leg components would be extruded section in aluminium alloy and the foot in die-cast aluminium bonded to the leg with adhesive, thus meeting the fire resistant requirements. The backrest and seat would be common to both chairs. To meet the user requirements the chairs would have to be strong and light, easy to clean and maintain within the agreed cost limits.

Design work

Robert Heritage then produced two prototype chairs, based on the two scale models which he had made for research purposes, incorporating the results of the research and following the agreed brief. The co-ordinating designer for Cunard selected the tourist version as the basis for both chairs. The outside of the seat and backrest of the tourist chair would be finished white with brilliant red upholstery inside; the first-class version would have the backrest and seat fully upholstered. Joining the seat and backrest to the leg assemblies for which an H-section was chosen, meant designing a method of fixing that avoided exterior screw and bolt fastenings. In each chair the seat assembly was designed with two pre-formed panels, the upper with a specially moulded cushion, upholstered on its top face only, and the lower, in the case of the tourist chair, covered with white plastic laminate, while the first class chair was upholstered on its outer face, the upper panel fitting neatly into the lower.

As with the BA chair before, the research and the designing were closely integrated. Product policy and the particular requirements of the time gave the designer a general conception of the chair, its overall appearance, its construction, material for the frame and production techniques. The details in each case were strongly influenced by the research carried out with a variety of specialists. As the design jelled, the designer drew together the solutions of the sub-problems, reconciling them one to another. The designers both of the BA and the *QE 2* chairs were able to turn their stringent analysis of function and technical opportunity to aesthetic advantage because they were determined to make both contribute to the realisation of the design objectives. The success with which this was done was due partly to the designers' ability to penetrate deeply into the essence of each problem and stretch the capability of technicians involved to the maximum, and partly to the close integration of the points of view of manager and designer. The

159

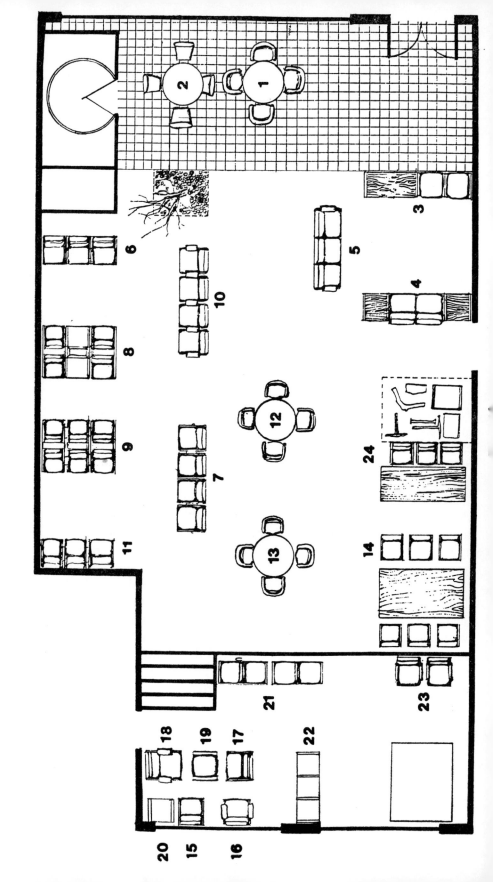

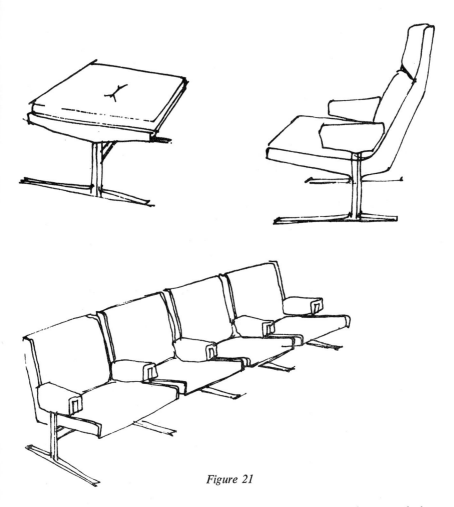

Figure 21

extent to which this was achieved in Race Furniture must be regarded as exceptional, but it can none the less stand as a model. To both designer and manager economy meant the elimination of waste—of material, of effort in manufacture, of time in the factory or in cleaning and maintenance. Economy meant value rather than cheapness, and it was the corner-stone of an elegant solution to a design problem. The Race method of researching a design requirement and bringing to bear upon it the wide range of expertise needed to meet it, illuminates the study of design for large firms who are committing vast resources of capital and plant to a particular design project. The essence of the designer–

161

manager relationship at Race is an object-lesson to others, but it will be achieved by more formal and systematic methods which are suited to the larger number of people involved and the inevitable fragmentation of responsibilities which in a big organisation a design manager must unite.

Results

Within its own terms of reference Race Furniture has been successful. For more than a generation it has been a viable concern, giving a healthy livelihood to those concerned in it. Race has not made large profits but management, designers and operatives have all derived great satisfaction from the progressive contribution the firm has made to the industry; some of their designs are classic in the history of modern furniture. These are assets to the well-being of an enterprise from which management can benefit in industrial relations.

Robert Heritage based a range of chairs, stools and tables for hotels, restaurant, airports and public areas on the *QE 2* design (see plate IV, facing p. 145). They could be single units or linked in a variety of combinations amounting in all to twenty-four units. Again these were aimed at the contract market and architects in particular. So the promotional material followed the previous pattern of folders of fine photographs and a factual leaflet giving straight-forward details and an environmental plan showing the units set out in a public room (figures 16 and 17).

Inevitably Race has been imitated. In the early days of the BA chair a firm accustomed to designing for wood produced a challenger but it did not appreciate the characteristics of metal construction, and the sectioning of the frame was different. Consequently the design was more complicated and more expensive, so it did not compete. This happened again with the same chair some fifteen years after its original production when a similar version was produced by an American firm, who made no bones about the chair's origin and eventually came to an arrangement with Race Furniture.

Because Race Furniture quickly established a reputation for design innovation their work was particularly interesting to architects and designers who gave it much publicity by introducing it into exhibition schemes and important public interiors. It was for the same reason interesting to editors of the magazine press. Consequently the firm was soon well known and much talked about; it became a point of reference at the advanced end of the trade. Jordan's own enthusiasm for what he was doing was infectious and itself generated interest. This prestige success was very important to the development of the firm, bringing it clients seeking development and a regular series of awards from the Design Council, the Milan Triennale and the Presidential Award for Design Management of the Royal Society of Arts. In the case of Race the product policy, the design and development initiative and the concentration on a narrow but profitable section of the contract market created a successful, although limited operation.

Noel Jordan himself stresses that his ability to adopt a policy of regular innovation depended to some extent on his not being a public company accountable to shareholders, nor had he family shareholders dependent upon him to sustain their income. It is axiomatic in our economy that a commercial enterprise must in the final analysis be profitable. If it is not, it stands no chance of being anything else. With profitability go other satisfactions which ensure the long-term stability of the firm. Undoubtedly those who have adopted a professional stance toward design, and used it as an aid to profitability, have derived at many levels satisfactions which contribute to pride in the job and in being part of the company. Increasingly managements realise that a successful organisation must generate social satisfaction as well as fat pay packets; in one sense design comes in this category.

In his address to the Royal Society of Arts on receiving its presidential award for design management, Mr Terence Conran, director and founder of Conran and Company Limited, said:

From the beginning design has been the mainspring of our business. It has an intense significance for us, an importance just as great as the profit motive might be in other companies. But in case we should sound too puritan about it, I should explain that part of the reason we have pursued a policy of good design is that we have profited from it.

Good design is of course, mainly logic with a small additive of aesthetics. We are constantly surprised that any company can proceed forward without it. After all, something that is rationally considered must therefore be well designed functionally, and if it is functionally correct then almost certainly it will be aesthetically pleasing too. If one

163

adds to these basic ingredients care in manufacture, efficient marketing and proper after-sales service, one should find that one has a product which outsells others lacking these essential virtues.

The manager does not have to choose between these satisfactions and profitability. They both go hand in hand and it is the manager's task to ensure that he receives both benefits from his management of the design process.

Conclusions

There is no mystique about design management; it is just rather difficult. It is difficult because it penetrates into so many departments of an organisation's activity and is concerned with their co-ordination. It is, therefore, a measure of management's general effectiveness and is a mirror of an organisation's health. A company's policy towards design reflects its attitude to nearly every activity. Even when these attitudes are clearly defined, and often they are not, they are difficult to interpret administratively and then to maintain against a constant erosion of day-to-day compromises. Design standards within a firm can be a visible indicator of standards of management. Low standards of design do not automatically indicate unprofitability, but they do reveal a neglect, on the part of management, of factors which in the long run may affect the wellbeing of the enterprise.

Design is not a once-for-all activity. The intensity depends on the type of product and the size of the enterprise, but in most concerns it is a continuing activity, affecting many departments, and it needs to be constantly related to productivity and marketing. If design work is not closely integrated with these two aspects, the design department will become isolated and eventually wither. A design department which is out on a limb cannot be expected to fulfil its vital function of ensuring that resources are used profitably.

The design policy of expanding businesses admits the constant awareness of change and the designers are concerned not only to meet change but also to anticipate it, so that the company's products and services are in line with the current needs of the market, thus helping to keep the firm in the forefront of competition. Change implies new design work and new designs should achieve improvement. To increase productivity, to reduce cost, to simplify maintenance, to engender satisfaction

165

externally and internally are the challenges set by management to designers today. Success goes to those who can combine technical skills and imaginative innovation to meet as fully as possible the customer's requirements, so that both the customer and the shareholders are pleasantly surprised. The attitude of the customer to the producer and his product will be substantially conditioned by the character and effectiveness of the firm's design policy. For this to be effective, on whatever scale, there must be constant vigilance and some imagination on the part of management, adequate budgets and positive conviction in the boardroom.

Although there is little disagreement among senior managers that the aim of the design process is to produce and give satisfaction to the producer in terms of economical production and profit, and to the user in terms of performance, convenience and even pleasure, the arguments begin when the means by which this aim is to be achieved have to be organised. This problem is not finally solved by merely appointing one or more professional designers, although this is essential as a company moves from amateur to professional status in matters of design. Having hired the skills appropriate to the marketing problem and the available resources, the essence of design management is to provide an organisation and a management style which will realise the range of satisfaction set out in the company's objectives.

Organisation

A successful organisation of design work depends basically on the distinguishing between the elements to which conventional administrative procedures can be applied and those to which creative stimulus is vital. There are always the twin dangers of allowing administration to squeeze the life out of the design department and then blaming it for a lack of successful ideas, and, on the other hand, failing to support the designers with a strong organisational framework, clear cut requirements and adequate status and budgets. The correct mixture is a matter of managerial judgement according to the particular case, whether it be an automatic milking machine or a range of fashion textiles. But in each case the basis for the judgement is a clear insight into the process of designing to ensure a smooth flow of information and ideas, and sufficient freedom to develop creative solutions within a systematic framework.

Most design systems divide logically into five phases: statement of

166

requirements, data collection, analysis and synthesis, evaluation, and communication of the selected solution in appropriate detail to all concerned. On the basis of the statement and the data, a design brief can be compiled, and this is the touchstone for the design activities. It is rare to achieve a complete statement of requirements, but lack of precision runs the risk of wastage at the critical stage of analysis and synthesis, with the result that it does not stand up to evaluation. Great managerial skill is required to specify comprehensively without inhibiting invention, innovation and creative design work at a later stage. In trying to overcome this the manager often tends to try and reconcile the conflict of requirements. This is not his function and to try to do so only confuses the issue; it is the task of the design activity. What the manager can do is to set the priority between one requirement and another; this can be exceedingly difficult and sometimes requires Board decisions.

From the standpoint of management the stage of analysis and synthesis is the most delicate. The areas of decision can be isolated and those who can make the decisions clearly identified, but the actual working out of viable solutions rests with the few people who need to be allowed to work in as creative a manner as possible. This small group requires every encouragement to think creatively and be exposed to external stimulus and ideas without becoming too diverted from the main task. Contact with other designers in a wide variety of fields, visits to factories abroad which are not direct competitors and familiarity with experimental work of all kinds are useful sources of ideas. It is not easy to judge what is relevant and what is not, but a liberal attitude is preferable. Successful designers, particularly in the consumer goods industries, are rarely backroom boys, and it is not in the interests of management to encourage them to be.

The manager can simplify design work considerably by drawing a clear distinction in the design brief between hard information capable of quantification and matters of conjecture in which imagination plays an important part. The aim will always be to extend the area of precise knowledge as widely as possible and to isolate the area of uncertainty which the designers will have to tackle. There are, by definition, relatively few design problems which are completely encompassed by precise knowledge. There is usually an area of uncertainty which has to be subjected to analysis using informed opinion, experience from similar situations and intuition. There is a tendency for this sector of the prob-

167

lem to become a Tom Tiddler's ground in which everyone regards his opinion to be as good as the next. This is not so and the manager can skilfully contrive that only informed opinion, from those qualified to give it, is sought and acted upon. This does not preclude the manager organising a brainstorming session when the situation is wide open in the early stages, but one well-timed session per project should be enough.

A whole series of decisions may depend on informed opinion rather than calculation, concerning form, the relationship of components, finishes and other appearance factors. If management supports informed opinion rather than prejudice, the other members of the team will soon recognise that it is informed and applied with skill. For example, both precise knowledge and experienced opinion are needed to decide the correct combination of light sources and surface treatments in order to create an effective environment for a drawing-office. So-called subjective judgements can contribute measurably to the success of a product, and every member of a design or production team should be clear which problems can be wholly analysed quantitively or statistically and which require this kind of judgement; and if the latter, who has the appropriate experience and ability to decide.

Design work tends to cut across the strictly pyramidal hierarchy and some organisation is usually needed to make those involved in the design process project-oriented. The product policy group will be biased in favour of the Board members, but this would not exclude the chief designer if he were not on the Board. Likewise the evaluation group will admit a strong marketing voice in addition to production and cost analysis. In the composition of a design team it is more important to allow the creative elements full play than to preserve a conventional seniority. At the production stage the interests which were paramount during designing will inevitably become subsidiaries. Such delicate transitions need handling with tact, and this is much more easily done if the management strategy is made clear in advance, by the formal charting of the progress of the project and the use of normal control methods. Most designers are glad to be relieved of this administrative burden so that they can concentrate on their professional task. A design department of any size needs a small administrative cell, but if that becomes a major preoccupation, it is probably a sign that management is failing to do its own job.

168

Marketing

A proper assessment of the relationship between design and marketing can be a vital part of a company's design policy. Most managers recognise that design has a direct bearing on sales, but this is often followed by the incorrect assumption that designers are only concerned with superficialities that might catch the eye of the customer, an attitude which confused the automobile industry and was in some measure corrected by the brilliant fusion of performance and convenience factors in Issigonis's design of the Mini. The appliance industries have suffered from the same limited interpretation until the consumer movement began to assert itself. Even in the least three-dimensional of goods such as textiles, design is in, not just on, a product. The process of designing begins with the conception of a product.

A design team needs precise knowledge of conditions which influence design for each particular market. This is more fundamental than just surveying what kind of designs are current best-sellers. Market research will go deeper than that if management want the design team to create original designs which can put the firm at the head of competition, rather than those which only reflect what is now selling, so that they merely join in at the tail end of the race. In a new market it is not usually enough to take the views of the agent or the retail buyer; it is desirable to include a detailed appreciation of the actual user's point of view. It is then possible to compare the real requirements of the market with the design characteristics of a product, and decide whether there is a commercial opportunity to promote the identical product. If not the next question is whether it is reasonable to re-design the product, taking into account the size of the market. It can be an advantage if designers occasionally visit overseas markets with a clear brief from management concerning what they are looking for, preferably as a final stage of a market research programme. In many markets of the world, competitors now have the same materials and processes at their disposal, consequently they have to aim at products which combine sophistication and simplification, and are elegant in both the scientific and aesthetic senses.

Fierce competition is obliging manufacturers to consider more and more the relationship between their products or services and their customers. Increasingly products are required for a precise environment,

169

a control room, a kitchen or a hospital; engineering goods have an operator and have to be cleaned and serviced; they are often used in conjunction with other equipment. Even the most enlightened customer cannot now be expected to specify fully the product which he requires, and it is no longer adequate to think only in terms of easy and economical production. Too narrow an interpretation of function will not produce an optimum solution which embraces all requirements of use through to presentation and corporate identity.

From the point of view of the customer for engineering goods a product is successfully designed when it suits its environment and its operators, and gives advantages in terms of man-hours, machine-hours, industrial welfare and fosters pride in the job. Basically the customer searches the market for machines to do their job efficiently, but he also expects them to be safe, convenient and good to look at. It is no longer commercially prudent to neglect these factors for which the studies of anthropometrics and ergonomics have established a field of reasonably precise knowledge where hitherto personal prejudice predominated.

The industrial designer is particularly qualified by training and experience to resolve these requirements of the customer, and he will argue for them when management evaluates a design solution. A design manager will always probe a salesman's statement that he is giving the customer what he wants. This may be partially true, but in an ideal situation where a manufacturer gives his customers something rather better than they realise they wanted, and at a competitive price, the prospects of profitability are greater. Designers can help to ensure that there is no waste in the use of materials and that techniques are used with maximum efficiency and economy, so that both men and machines are as productive as possible, thus keeping the price competitive.

Market requirements for goods which are sold through a retailer are often more complex. Preferences may seem to vary markedly from one region to another. For appliances regulations and dimensions may be radically different in export markets. In some consumer goods the retailer may require distinctive characteristics to be obvious as sales points; at the same time he may refer to the predominance of an international style in design which makes price and quality the overriding factors in his choice of supplier. It is in this retailed merchandise that a design policy is particularly important. A progressive policy is needed to design goods of a distinction which puts them in the forefront of an international design trend or gives them an apparently exclusive character or price advantage. These aspects are difficult to put into a design brief but they are as important as the requirements for safety and economical distribution and convenient storage by the retailers, for point of sale presentation which will give impact and identity, sales and instruction literature of quality and character compatible with the product.

In order to compete on the shelf with other retailed products, a design brief will stress the co-ordination of advertising and other promotion with the appearance of product and pack; it will require their integration with the corporate identity programme all along the line. These are marketing tools created by the skilled use of design services.

Dealing with Designers

No matter how well the basic data is collected or the initial statement of requirements prepared or the cost or production factors appreciated, a vital part of the success of a product will depend on the creative ability of the designer. Briefs and statements and analyses do not of themselves ensure improved products and services. The stimulation of a creative approach to problems should rank equally with the application of formal methods of problem-solving and the cultivation of sound judgement in design matters. Consequently the development of a productive as well as orderly ambience in the design department may take up a fair slice of a manager's time. If the time spent produces results, all is well, but when the results are disappointing over a reasonable period the management style or the designers need changing. Designers cannot be dragooned into creative work, nor can they be left to moulder on their own. Experienced management realises that good designers do not grow on trees; searching for them is an exacting business and when found they need cultivation. Fortunately, there are an increasing number of highly professional designers capable of carrying out creative and rewarding work.

The wide span of the designers' interest in performance, maintenance, convenience, aesthetic appeal, packaging, print and presentation can make problems for management. The very roving nature of their work may cause embarrassment because their overall concern with so many aspects may make them suspect to other specialists who may feel that

171

designers should be discouraged by management from poaching. The proliferation of specialists is one of the great managerial problems. Knowledge has become more and more specialised and fragmented and the reputation of the expert has increasingly depended on his finding some tight little island of expertise where he can rule undisputed. In medicine the general practitioner is rapidly being reduced to a booking-clerk for the regional hospital boards, whereas if a doctor isolates an anopheles peculiar to the northern province of Ashanti, the odds are that his career is made as a recognised authority.

In industry management has to decide who, among the ever-expanding hierarchy of specialists, is going to co-ordinate these increasingly divergent ends. A method of achieving synthesis out of all these specialisations is needed, and a competence of people to practice the co-ordination. The manager is only too aware that merely to call in one more expert may delay rather than hasten a solution. In this context he may well ask whether the designer is a specialist or a co-ordinator. Designers often like to look upon themselves as specialists enjoying the acclaim that goes with expertise, although they realise that their skill is both analytical and synthetic. There is no clear-cut answer; basically the designer is a specialist in the design process. Management can exploit this as a basis for his status. At the same time his function is predominantly co-ordination in many industrial situations.

Management can take a flexible attitude towards the problem. In problems where the solution lies largely within the span of subjects in which the chief designer is experienced, he can be the co-ordinator of the product programme, but in firms where the design solutions lie more within other disciplines such as precision engineering, the co-ordinator could come from that discipline, with the professional designer providing specialist skills. The essential point is to avoid a string of specialists without any authoritative and effective co-ordinator. Those who have training and experience from whatever discipline in synthesising problems will be strong candidates; this puts the professional designer in a favourable but not decisive position for the role. In either case designers can be encouraged to heighten their appreciation of all aspects of production and marketing so that the design process can be applied wherever it is appropriate and not merely looked upon by management as an envelope in which to present a product or service.

An experienced designer seldom believes that he is omniscient when

172

he is dealing with specialists such as engineers or salesmen. He will be more concerned to explain to other members of the team what he is trying to achieve, and to emphasise his rational approach to matters which some specialist may regard as the province only of personal opinion. Human reactions to such design factors as colour and form may seem quite unpredictable to some people; they may even feel that their reactions are an expression of personal liberty. But to the designer a whole series of behavioural patterns may be predictable within broad limits and they can be explained quite rationally by someone who is properly informed on the limitations and potentialities of human perception. To do this adequately designers themselves must be perceptive.

In considering the composition of the design team there are two personal characteristics which designers should have. The discipline imposed by modern industrial production makes a well-developed intelligence vital. If it is lacking a designer will have difficulty in keeping pace with his technical colleagues and this will inhibit him and prevent his asking effective questions. The ability to evaluate information from many sources and to explain ideas or conclusions is also important. Such qualifications justify adequate status so that designers can collect and communicate ideas without obstruction, arguing their case among equals while retaining their creative enthusiasm. Useful results are often lost after appointing a well-qualified designer because he lacks the status and managerial support which he needs in order to become effective. Secondly, designers should bring to the team a positive inventiveness, relevant to the problem. Designers trained in art schools may be adept at this and it needs to be married to an appreciation of technology. Designing is an art, often science based, rather than a sophisticated calculation, even when computers are used to manipulate the data. Given encouragement designers will create opportunities for extending their experience, but a repressive managerial hand will circumscribe them to the detriment of their work. The environment in which they work should be stimulating and reflect as far as possible the standards which the company wishes to be evident in their finished products. Some firms attach great importance to this, siting design departments separately from the main factory, although this may have the disadvantage of their becoming remote from production. More important, perhaps, is to have space and freedom from disturbance provided they can get together quickly with other designers and technicians when they are working out ideas. A well-planned and equipped design department is one step towards professional rather than makeshift results. Managers may find that, contrary to their instinct for fair play, elitism rather than egalitarianism fosters creativity. It pays, as in other activities, to have a clear understanding between managers and designers concerning administrative facilities, timetables and costs. When dealing with consultant designers a detailed contract will avoid misunderstandings concerning who provides what services, requirements, date lines and costs. It is always preferable to work out the details in advance rather than deal with them as they crop up, and to envisage the possibility of breaking off the work if necessary at an agreed point, perhaps at the end of the first phase. Design is a professional business and should be approached professionally on both sides. There are several ways of paying designers and the method appropriate to the case should be worked out in advance. Finally there is the question of copyright to be settled. As the success of design work so often depends on a sensitivity to detail, it usually pays to sustain the designer's interest right through to completion.

Since design work is concerned with improvement and penetrates deeply into the activities of many departments, there may often be opportunities for management consultants to work with designers. By the same token an alert manager may perceive that some aspect of a management consultant's report points to a design programme. The work of the two consultants may be complementary, with the design manager as link man. The latter holds a key position in the expansion of an organisation and this should stand him in good stead for further responsibility. In particular he will gain insight into the nature of creativity and this in turn will make him aware of the kind of people who have creative potential. He will not be distracted by their patterns of behaviour, remembering the connection between progress and 'unreasonable people' detected by Bernard Shaw, which establishes the relatedness of previously unrelated metrices.

Corporate Identity

Inevitably aspects of corporate identity have been touched upon in all previous sections, and this reflects the constant awareness the manager needs to have of total design, if the maximum impact of design work is to be obtained. An investigation into corporate identity can reveal many opportunities for standardisation, rationalisation, variety reduction and simplification. When embarking on such a programme the manager first wants to survey the extent of the total project and then divide it into manageable stages, making sure that each aspect brings an identifiable benefit to some sector of the enterprise. He will use the eyes of his designers to discover how the firm's resources may be applied in new ways, and how the administrative structure may be more aptly related to the operations which actually take place. It is the ideal opportunity to rethink old procedures and analyse them from a fresh point of view, constantly assessing whether the outward and visible signs of the organisation indicate an inward and effective grace.

In many cases the starting-point will be print which is an area wide open to rationalisation and co-ordination. Service industries can particularly benefit from design skills applied to all aspects of print as the case studies show, but the exercise requires designers capable of penetrating into the functional requirements of the printed matter. The term 'house style' only suggests the surface of the problem. The corporate identity on the other hand springs from a great variety of fundamental forces. The manager may find difficulty in persuading some of his colleagues that it has more than marginal value, but he should be able to convince them that in a competitive market it is a margin which may prove decisive in tipping the scales of customer preference in their favour.

The wide span of the activity and its vulnerability make an effective system of control essential. Firstly, the manager will avoid biting off more than he can chew and secondly, he will establish clear guide lines of control without stifling a desirable degree of flexibility as circumstances change. Above all he will insist on a professional approach to the subject by professionals, of whom a design consultant experienced in the art will certainly be one, resisting all temptations from the accountants to do it on the cheap with artistic amateurs. Corporate identity requires a volatile mixture of method and imagination. To settle for less may well be to throw good money after bad. Ultimately both aspects may be enshrined in a design manual. This will not however be regarded as sacred; it will need regular re-appraisal and inevitable modification;

175

it can easily become a sacred cow, and equally counter-productive if it does so. The study of successful cases suggests that a highly competitive trading situation emphasises the need for an effective corporate identity. In that situation the firm's design organisation will have a strong link with marketing.

Short Reading List

Archer, L. Bruce, *Systematic Methods for Designers*, Design Council, 1965.

Blake, John E. (Ed.), *A Management Guide to Corporate Identity*, Design Council, 1971.

Blake, John E. (Ed.), *Designing for European Markets*, Design Council, 1972.

Croney, J., *Anthropometrics for Designers*, Batsford, 1971.

Davis, Alec, *Graphics: Design into Production*, Faber, 1973.

Falk, Roger, *The Business of Management*, Penguin, 1970.

Goslett, D., *Professional Practice for Designers*, Batsford, 1971.

Henrion & Parkin, *Design Co-ordination and Corporate Image*, Studio Vista, 1967.

Jones, J. Christopher, *Design Methods*, Wiley, 1970.

OECD, *Design Departments*, Paris, OECD.

Pilditch, James, & Scott, Douglas, *The Business of Product Design*, Business Books, 1965.

Pye, D., *The Nature of Design*, Studio Vista, 1964.

Russell-Clarke, A. D., *Copyright in Industrial Design*, Sweet & Maxwell, 1968.

177

Index